Finishing Touches

DOLLS HOUSE DO-IT-YOURSELF

Finishing Touches

Jane Harrop

David & Charles

To Mum and Dad, with love

A DAVID & CHARLES BOOK
David & Charles is a subsidiary of F&W (UK) Ltd.,
an F&W Publications Inc. company

First published in the UK in 2004

Distributed in North America
by F&W Publications, Inc.
4700 East Galbraith Road
Cincinnati, OH 45236
1-800-289-0963

A catalogue record for this book is available from the British Library.

ISBN 0 7153 1794 6 paperback

Printed in Singapore by KHL Printing Co Pte Ltd
for David & Charles
Brunel House   Newton Abbot   Devon

Executive Editor Cheryl Brown
Editor Jennifer Proverbs
Art Editor Prudence Rogers
Book Designer Sarah Underhill
Production Controller Ros Napper
Project Editor Lin Clements
Photographer Karl Adamson

Visit our website at www.davidandcharles.co.uk

David & Charles books are available from all good bookshops;
alternatively you can contact our Orderline on (0) 1626 334555
or write to us at FREEPOST EX2110, David & Charles Direct,
Newton Abbot TQ12 4ZZ (no stamp required UK mainland).

DOLLS HOUSE DO-IT-YOURSELF

Finishing Touches

Contents

Introduction

I have been making miniatures now for ten years and what started as a hobby is now my part-time job: I sell my work to collectors and teach adult education classes on making dolls' house miniatures. This book guides you through making miniature ornamental and decorative interior accessories in one-twelfth scale, through step-by-step instructions and photographs (actual size where possible). There is a huge range of projects to make and although they have been grouped by era or style, many can be made for inclusion into other periods.

To help you with this, each project is introduced with a short history and illustrated variations are provided throughout to suggest how a project could be adapted to suit another period.

The first chapter visits the Elizabethan era, from the mid 16th century through to the beginning of the 17th, a time that saw prosperous merchants and politicians building homes to display their wealth, although furniture and accessories were sparse, even in the largest homes.

The mid Georgian period (1760–90) was the age of

elegance, introduced by Robert Adam and his associates who brought classical elements of style into architecture and interiors.

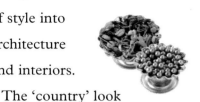

The 'country' look evolved into a charming, rustic style particularly popular during the 19th century. It originated in rural communities in the homes of those who weren't able to keep up with the latest vogues and fashions.

The Victorian era (1830–1901) was a time when piety, moral issues and the importance of family life was coupled with a love of the home. The industrial revolution gave rise to factories and mass production, resulting in affordable furnishings and decorative accessories.

The final chapter focuses on the magic of Christmas time during the Edwardian period (1901–14), when the upper and expanding middle classes delighted in filling their homes with attractive Christmas decorations.

I hope that you will find my choice of projects in this book both stimulating and satisfying. Whether you are seeking to add period furniture or stylish interior decorations to your miniature home, I am sure you will find the perfect finishing touches here.

Conversion Chart

All the projects in this book are one-twelfth scale, i.e., one inch in miniature is equal to one foot in full size (which is why many miniaturists still work to imperial measurements). In general most materials and tools for making miniatures are sold in imperial sizes, although some suppliers are now using metric measurements. The table below provides a guide to converting metric to imperial and vice versa, giving conversions that are relevant to this book. In practice, items may not be sold to their exact equivalent, for example a $1/32$in drill bit is sold in metric as 0.8 not 0.79, so very small degrees of measurement in metric have been rounded up or down.

Inch	Millimetre
$1/64$	0.4
$1/32$	0.8
$3/64$	1.2
$1/16$	1.6
$3/32$	2.4
$1/8$	3.2
$3/16$	4.8
$1/4$	6.3
$3/8$	9.5
$1/2$	12.7
$5/8$	15.9
$3/4$	19.0
$7/8$	22.0
1	25.4

Materials and Equipment

This section describes the basic materials and equipment you will need to complete the projects. They are readily available from craft and model shops but if you have difficulty in sourcing any of the items refer to Suppliers on page 63. Read through a project before you begin to ensure you have all the materials and equipment needed. There is also important safety advice on page 11.

Wood

Some of the projects are made of wood. The type of wood used is stated in each project but can be substituted if desired. Keep to the same wood type during a project for best results.

Bass wood A white-coloured wood with a fine, straight grain and an ideal substitute for obechi wood.

Jelutong wood A straw-coloured wood with a closed grain, ideal for small, detailed woodworking.

Obechi wood A pale yellow-coloured wood with an open grain. It is one of the lightest hardwoods available, making it ideal for sawing and cutting.

Wood dowel Cylindrical wood available in various diameters.

Bass wood

Jelutong wood

Obechi wood

Wood dowel

Woodworking Tools

These tools will make working with wood accurate, safe and simple.

Drills Mini electric drills are supplied with fine drill bits. They are more expensive than a hand-held pin vice (see below) but are quicker.

Mitre cutters These are basically scissors for wood and will cut and mitre strip wood up to $\frac{1}{2}$in thick. They are used as an alternative to a saw and mitre block.

Pin files These have fine, shaped heads for intricate shaping and sanding.

Pin vice A pin vice is used for drilling through wood and will hold extremely fine drill bits up to $\frac{1}{8}$in diameter.

Right-angled gluing jig A frame (easily made at home) with two fixed sides set at right angles which enables an object being glued to be held square.

Sandpaper Essential for shaping, smoothing and distressing wood. Use fine-grade sandpaper for projects at this scale.

Saw and mitre block A junior hacksaw or razor saw are used with a small mitre block to cut and mitre strip wood (see page 12). They are used as an alternative to mitre cutters and will also cut brass tube.

Right-angled gluing jig

Sandpaper

Pin vice

Pin file

Saw and mitre block

Mitre cutters

Colouring Mediums, Glues and Varnishes

Various colouring mediums and glues are used in the projects – see also Basic Techniques page 12.

3-D gloss varnish A liquid that produces a raised, glossy finish when dry. It is often used as a rubber-stamping accessory.

Metallic pastes Wax-based pastes, also known as gilt creams, can be applied sparingly to a painted surface to give the appearance of age and depth. Metallic shoe polish can be used as an alternative.

Paints These are available in a wide range, either water-based or oil-based. Water-based acrylic paints are recommended for most projects as they are non-toxic and easy to work with. Glass and enamel paints are also available in acrylics. Several of the projects require oil-based spray paints (see safety tips on page 11).

Paintbrushes Artist's paintbrushes are available in a range of sizes ideal for painting miniatures.

Shoe polish This is used as a wax-based wood stain and polish combined (see Basic Techniques page 12).

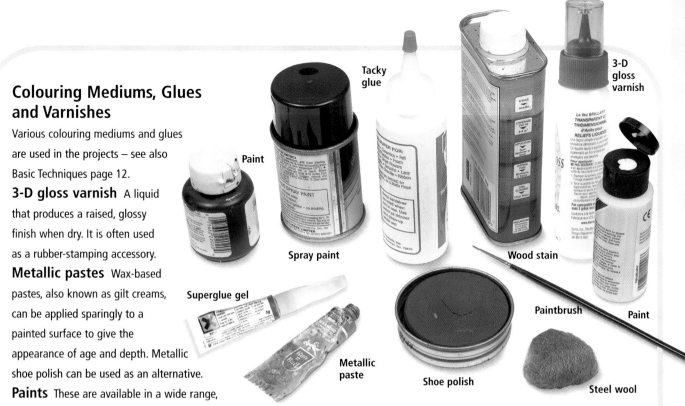

Paint

Tacky glue

3-D gloss varnish

Spray paint

Wood stain

Superglue gel

Paintbrush

Paint

Metallic paste

Shoe polish

Steel wool

Steel wool Use fine-grade wire to apply shoe polish to wood.

Superglue gel This strong glue is useful as it bonds instantly.

Tacky glue This non-toxic water-based glue dries clear, strong and flexible. It is particularly suited to wood, paper, card and fabric. Thick or mighty tacky glue is recommended for best results.

Wood stain A water-based or oil-based colouring applied to wood with a soft cloth. Use water-based wood stains to achieve distressed paint effects (see Basic Techniques page 12).

Basic Crafting Tools

There are some general crafting tools that you will find useful for many of the projects.

Craft knife An essential tool for cutting wood and card. Model-maker's knives with replaceable blades are preferable to Stanley knives. Always use with a cutting mat and steel ruler.

Cutting mat This is a must when cutting with a craft knife, to protect working surfaces.

Ruler A 12in steel ruler graduated in $\frac{1}{16}$in is an essential basic tool.

Scissors Small sharp scissors are essential for cutting paper and templates.

Paper punches Several of the projects use paper punches, available in a wide variety of shapes and sizes for the craft worker.

Pliers A useful tool for holding, cutting and bending wire.

Quilling tool A small, hand-held tool used to coil quilling paper.

Wire cutters A tool used specifically to cut wire.

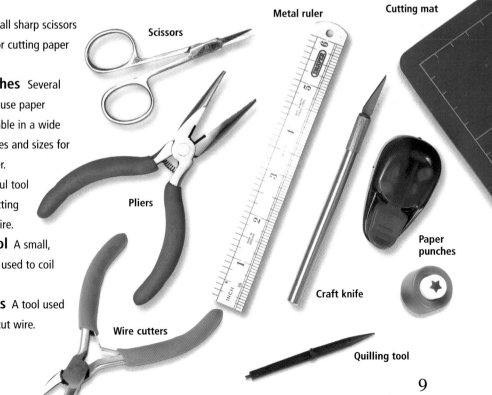

Scissors

Metal ruler

Cutting mat

Pliers

Craft knife

Paper punches

Wire cutters

Quilling tool

9

Specialist Materials

This list is a useful illustrated glossary and is arranged alphabetically. It describes many of the other items used to complete the projects, some of which may be unfamiliar to you.

Beads A variety of beads are used in the projects. Specific details of the beads required are given for each project.

Belaying pins A model ship-building component available in wood in various sizes from model shops.

Brass pins Available in various sizes from miniature hardware specialists.

Brass sheet Available from model shops. A cheaper alternative is the inside of a tomato purée tube.

Brass tube A hollow tube available in a range of diameters from model shops and cut using a mitre block and junior hacksaw.

Bunka Perhaps better known as lampshade fringing, this can be purchased either as fringing or tassels from haberdashery (notions) stores.

Canvas Two types of needlework canvas are used in some projects – tapestry canvas and suit interlining canvas.

Centre cane Used in basket making and available from specialist outlets in various thicknesses. It is known as round reed cane in the USA.

Clear plastic tube Often used to cover the bristles on new artist's paintbrushes.

Cocktail sticks A substitute for $1/16$in hardwood dowel.

Cold porcelain A non-toxic modelling material made from a mixture of PVA glue, cornflour and a preservative. It is most often used for cake decoration.

Double column Model ship-building component, available in wood from most good model shops.

Eyelets These are measured by the narrow opening at the top of the eyelet. Straight-ended ones are used in the projects rather than serrated ones.

Filigrees and findings Metal egg-decorating components, including scrolls, spokes, frames, decorative caps and up-eyes have been used in some projects.

Floral tape This is normally used to bind flowers and leaves together in cake decoration.

Flower shades Plastic flower shades from egg decorating or jewellery suppliers.

Jewellery findings These are metal jewellery-making components, including head pins, bead caps and pendant frames.

Paper balls Compact-shaped paper balls used in various crafts.

Peel-off motifs

Brass tube

Brass sheet

Scenic scatter

Cold porcelain

Bunka (lampshade fringing)

Waxed thread

Clear plastic tube

Belaying pins

Paper ball

Stamens

Beads

Double columns

Brass pins

Cocktail sticks

Colouring Mediums, Glues and Varnishes

Various colouring mediums and glues are used in the projects – see also Basic Techniques page 12.

3-D gloss varnish A liquid that produces a raised, glossy finish when dry. It is often used as a rubber-stamping accessory.

Metallic pastes Wax-based pastes, also known as gilt creams, can be applied sparingly to a painted surface to give the appearance of age and depth. Metallic shoe polish can be used as an alternative.

Paints These are available in a wide range, either water-based or oil-based. Water-based acrylic paints are recommended for most projects as they are non-toxic and easy to work with. Glass and enamel paints are also available in acrylics. Several of the projects require oil-based spray paints (see safety tips on page 11).

Paintbrushes Artist's paintbrushes are available in a range of sizes ideal for painting miniatures.

Shoe polish This is used as a wax-based wood stain and polish combined (see Basic Techniques page 12).

Steel wool Use fine-grade wire to apply shoe polish to wood.

Superglue gel This strong glue is useful as it bonds instantly.

Tacky glue This non-toxic water-based glue dries clear, strong and flexible. It is particularly suited to wood, paper, card and fabric. Thick or mighty tacky glue is recommended for best results.

Wood stain A water-based or oil-based colouring applied to wood with a soft cloth. Use water-based wood stains to achieve distressed paint effects (see Basic Techniques page 12).

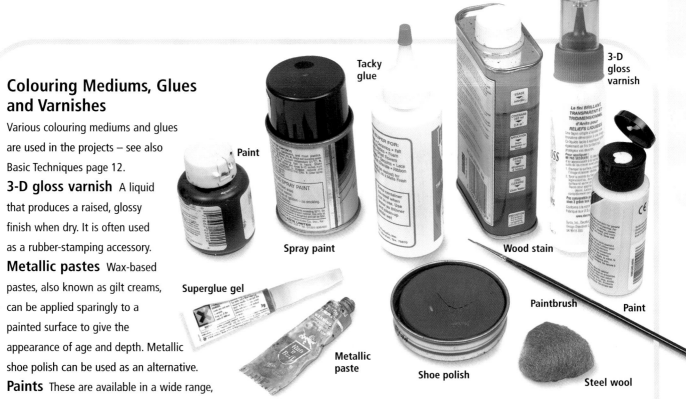

Paint · Tacky glue · Spray paint · 3-D gloss varnish · Superglue gel · Wood stain · Metallic paste · Paintbrush · Paint · Shoe polish · Steel wool

Basic Crafting Tools

There are some general crafting tools that you will find useful for many of the projects.

Craft knife An essential tool for cutting wood and card. Model-maker's knives with replaceable blades are preferable to Stanley knives. Always use with a cutting mat and steel ruler.

Cutting mat This is a must when cutting with a craft knife, to protect working surfaces.

Ruler A 12in steel ruler graduated in $^1/_{16}$in is an essential basic tool.

Scissors Small sharp scissors are essential for cutting paper and templates.

Paper punches Several of the projects use paper punches, available in a wide variety of shapes and sizes for the craft worker.

Pliers A useful tool for holding, cutting and bending wire.

Quilling tool A small, hand-held tool used to coil quilling paper.

Wire cutters A tool used specifically to cut wire.

Scissors · Metal ruler · Cutting mat · Pliers · Craft knife · Wire cutters · Paper punches · Quilling tool

Specialist Materials

This list is a useful illustrated glossary and is arranged alphabetically. It describes many of the other items used to complete the projects, some of which may be unfamiliar to you.

Beads A variety of beads are used in the projects. Specific details of the beads required are given for each project.

Belaying pins A model ship-building component available in wood in various sizes from model shops.

Brass pins Available in various sizes from miniature hardware specialists.

Brass sheet Available from model shops. A cheaper alternative is the inside of a tomato purée tube.

Brass tube A hollow tube available in a range of diameters from model shops and cut using a mitre block and junior hacksaw.

Bunka Perhaps better known as lampshade fringing, this can be purchased either as fringing or tassels from haberdashery (notions) stores.

Canvas Two types of needlework canvas are used in some projects – tapestry canvas and suit interlining canvas.

Centre cane Used in basket making and available from specialist outlets in various thicknesses. It is known as round reed cane in the USA.

Clear plastic tube Often used to cover the bristles on new artist's paintbrushes.

Cocktail sticks A substitute for $^1/_{16}$in hardwood dowel.

Cold porcelain A non-toxic modelling material made from a mixture of PVA glue, cornflour and a preservative. It is most often used for cake decoration.

Double column Model ship-building component, available in wood from most good model shops.

Eyelets These are measured by the narrow opening at the top of the eyelet. Straight-ended ones are used in the projects rather than serrated ones.

Filigrees and findings Metal egg-decorating components, including scrolls, spokes, frames, decorative caps and up-eyes have been used in some projects.

Floral tape This is normally used to bind flowers and leaves together in cake decoration.

Flower shades Plastic flower shades from egg decorating or jewellery suppliers.

Jewellery findings These are metal jewellery-making components, including head pins, bead caps and pendant frames.

Paper balls Compact-shaped paper balls used in various crafts.

Peel-off motifs

Brass tube

Brass sheet

Scenic scatter

Bunka (lampshade fringing)

Cold porcelain

Waxed thread

Clear plastic tube

Belaying pins

Stamens

Paper ball

Beads

Double columns

Brass pins

Cocktail sticks

Paper ribbon A fine, creased paper which is commonly used to make bows for floral arrangements.

Pastel paper A strong-grained artist's paper available in a range of colours.

Peel-off motifs Adhesive-backed motifs mostly used for decorating greetings cards.

Polymer clay Modelling clay that can be baked in domestic ovens to make items that are solid and long lasting.

Quilling paper Narrow strips of paper, available in a range of colours and widths.

Ribbon Silk and organdie ribbon are used in some projects. Both are fine and manageable and available in a range of colours and widths.

Scenic scatter This is a model railway material used to make scenery.

Stamens These are normally used in the centre of a flower in cake decorating and are available in a range of sizes and colours.

Water-slide transfers (decals) Designs used to decorate a wide range of items. Separate the transfer from the paper backing by soaking in water for several minutes. Miniature transfers are often used in egg decorating.

Wire Jewellery-making wire and florist's stub wire are available in various gauges. Some projects use paper-covered wire, which is commonly used in cake decoration.

Waxed thread A thread treated with wax, often used in jewellery making.

Safety tips

Be aware that all tools have sharp cutting edges and should be used and stored safely.

When sanding wood *always* wear a dust mask to prevent inhalation of fine dust particles.

Ensure good ventilation when using spray paints, oil- and wax-based products and superglue.

Always wash your hands thoroughly at the end of each session.

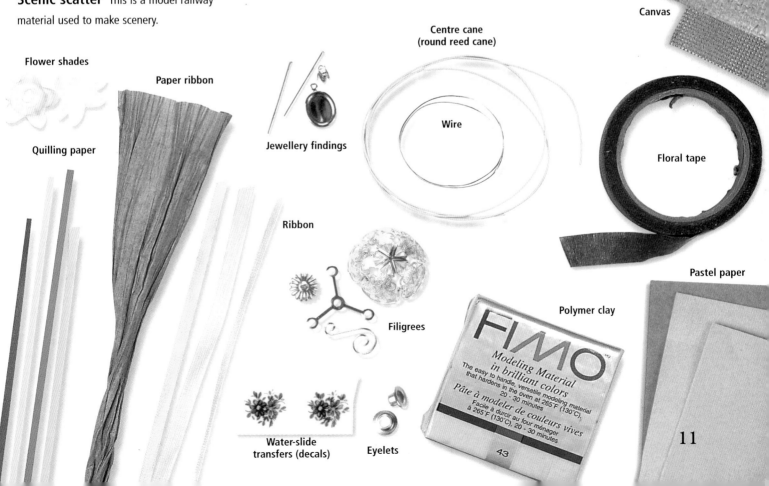

Flower shades

Paper ribbon

Quilling paper

Jewellery findings

Centre cane
(round reed cane)

Wire

Canvas

Floral tape

Ribbon

Filigrees

Water-slide
transfers (decals)

Eyelets

Polymer clay

Pastel paper

11

Basic Techniques

This section covers the commonly used basic techniques required to make the projects in this book and should be referred to when necessary.

Using Colouring Mediums

The projects use various colouring mediums, including water-based acrylic paints, shoe polish and wood stain.

Paints Apply acrylic water-based paints with an artist's paintbrush: medium (approx. size 6) and fine (approx. size 000) are needed for some projects. Several of the projects use oil-based spray or enamel paints; follow the manufacturer's safety instructions when using these products.

Shoe polish Apply shoe polish to wood using fine-gauge wire wool and buff up to a sheen with clean wire wool or a cloth. Avoid using polish on edges to be glued, as the bond will not be as strong.

Wood stain Apply wood stain to wood using a soft cloth and use sparingly as too much can warp the wood. Stain parts before assembly, allowing them to dry completely.

Distressing Techniques

A distressing technique is used to imitate age and wear and tear to a surface. Wood in particular responds well to such treatments.

Make up the project following the instructions and paint with water-based acrylic paint. Sand the item in places where natural wear and tear would occur, to reveal the wood. Cover the whole article with a light water-based wood stain such as antique pine or medium oak. Remove the stain from the wood in accessible areas with a damp cloth. The stain will settle in the cracks and colour the bare wood, mimicing worn paint and grime.

Use water-based wood stain and shoe polish sparingly to achieve aged finishes on other materials, such as paper, card and fabric.

Cutting Wood

Use a craft knife, mitre cutters or a saw to cut wood, cutting so the grain runs in line with the sides that have the longest measurement. Sand and polish wood following the grain.

Chamfering This means creating an angle at the edge of the piece of wood. Hold the piece of wood upright (at a slight angle) above fine-grade sandpaper, with the edge to be chamfered facing down. Sand the edge in small sweeping motions in the same direction, until you achieve the correct angle. Two angles, 45 and 60 degrees, are drawn here.

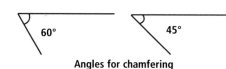

Angles for chamfering

Mitring This means cutting the ends of two wood pieces to an angle of 45 degrees so they can be fitted together to make a right-angled joint. Use a mitre block and razor saw, positioning the saw in the slits of the mitre block to cut diagonally through the wood. Press the wood against the guide of the mitre cutters to achieve a 45-degree angle cut.

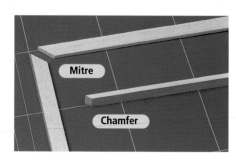

Mitre

Chamfer

Using a mitre block and saw

Framing

Mitring the ends of four strips of wood and then joining them together makes a frame. Each pair of pieces should be the same length. Position the corresponding size lengths opposite each other in a right-angled gluing jig (see page 8) and glue together.

When mitring picture frame moulding, make sure the recess on the back of the wood runs with the shortest length of mitred wood strip.

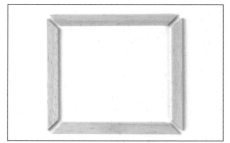

Making a frame with mitred wood strips

Using Templates

Some of the projects have templates for you to use and these can be found on pages 61–62. Black and white templates should be photocopied for accuracy, although they may be traced with pencil and tracing paper if preferred. Colour templates should be reproduced either by colour photocopying on to white paper or card or by scanning the image into a computer and then printing on photo-quality card or paper.

Tudor Times

Wooden Stool

During Tudor times the most usual type of seating at mealtimes for the majority of the household was either stools or benches (see also pages 18 and 31). They were often simply constructed out of oak and placed against a wall, with the wall used as a backrest.

You will need

$^3/_{32}$in thick obechi sheet wood,
   1$^1/_2$in x 1in for seat

$^1/_4$in x $^1/_8$in obechi strip wood:
   two 1$^1/_8$in lengths for long seat supports
   two $^5/_8$in lengths for short seat supports

$^1/_8$in x $^1/_8$in obechi strip wood:
   four 1$^3/_8$in lengths for legs
   two 1$^1/_8$in lengths for long leg supports
   two $^5/_8$in lengths for short leg supports

Oak-coloured shoe polish

Steel wool

Tacky glue

Variation

This country-style version of the stool has a pierced finger hole so it can be picked up easily. Drill three $^3/_{64}$in holes centrally along the middle of the seat and then use a craft knife and sandpaper to clean the drilled section. The leg supports are positioned $^3/_{16}$in from the end of each leg.

1 Sand each of the wooden components using fine-grade sandpaper. Use steel wool to apply an oak-coloured shoe polish to colour and polish each of the wood pieces (see Basic Techniques page 12).

2 Place two legs, a short seat support and a short leg support (positioned $^1/_{16}$in from the end of each leg) in a right-angled gluing jig (see page 8) and glue together. Repeat the procedure with the remaining two legs and short supports.

3 Once dry, take the leg constructions and place sideways in the gluing jig. Position and glue a long seat support and long leg support in between the leg structures and in line with the other supports. Repeat the procedure with the remaining wood pieces.

4 Position and glue the frame centrally on to the underside of the seat. If you wish achieve the appearance of age and dirt on the polished surface, rub a small amount of black shoe polish into some areas and buff with wire wool.

Torchère

For many people during Tudor times, the light from a domestic fire would have been the only source of illumination. The wealthy used wax candles held in various types of candleholders. Heavy, floor-standing torchères were usually made out of wood or iron and often had a pricket, a spike fitting in the centre of the pan, which held the candle upright. See also the candlesticks on page 37.

You will need

$^{1}/_{16}$in diameter brass tube,
   $3^{1}/_{2}$in length

$^{9}/_{16}$in diameter aluminium
   dinner plate

Gold-plated head pin, 1in length

Three gold-plated scrolls,
   $^{3}/_{4}$in long

White cake candle

Pewter enamel spray paint

Superglue gel

Variation

This candlestick is a smaller version of the torchère and is made following the same instructions. Use a $1^{1}/_{4}$in length of $^{1}/_{16}$in diameter brass tube, a 6mm gold-plated bead cap, three $^{7}/_{16}$in long gold-plated scrolls and a slim white cake candle.

1 Place the aluminium plate upside-down and drill a hole centrally through the middle using a $^{3}/_{64}$in drill bit. Cut the head end off the gold-plated head pin so it measures $^{1}/_{8}$in. Keep the opposite end as this is used to make the pricket.

2 Use superglue gel to secure the head pin into one end of the brass tube and the straight end of the pin (the pricket) into the opposite end. The pricket should protrude by $^{3}/_{8}$in. Glue the scrolls on to the end of the brass tube, allowing each one to dry before gluing the next. (Alternatively, solder the scrolls on for a stronger join.) Put the plate through the spike to rest on top of the tube and glue into place. Once dry, spray the torchère with pewter enamel spray paint.

Cut and prepare a white cake candle (see step 2, page 37) to $^{1}/_{2}$in long and insert on to the pricket.

15

Fighting Axe

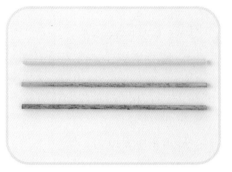

Arms and armour made by skilled craftsmen decorated the walls of many grand houses during the Tudor period. Most weapons were made with the aim of killing or injuring, however, some were made more as costume items than weapons. Others were created using precious metals and finished ornately, to display the wealth and position of the owner.

You will need

Thin card for black and white photocopying

$^3/_{32}$in diameter hardwood dowel, $3^1/_2$in length

Dark brown and black shoe polish

Steel wool

Silver and black water-based acrylic paints

Tacky glue

Variation

Make a spear like this using the axe instructions. Use a 6in length of $^1/_{16}$in diameter hardwood dowel and photocopy the spearhead templates on page 62.

1 Photocopy the axe template on page 62 on to thin card and use small, sharp scissors to cut around the outline. Use a craft knife and a ruler to score along the line between the two 'blades'. Fold the card so the scored line is on the inside.

2 To make the shaft, take the hardwood dowel and use steel wool to apply a dark brown shoe polish, followed by black shoe polish to colour and polish the wood (see Basic Techniques page 12).

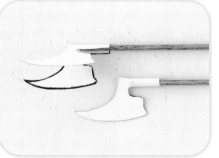

3 Position and glue the end of the shaft inside the shaped card as shown. Rub tacky glue over the inside of one of the card blades and press the other into place on top. If the blades are not exactly equal, trim to match once dry.

4 Mix a small amount of black and silver water-based acrylic paints to make a dark silver colour. Apply a thin layer of paint to the axe head using a small paintbrush. Repeat the procedure until totally covered.

Leather Bucket

Leather was a popular material for making containers for liquids during medieval times and continued to be used through to the Tudor period. Leather had the advantage of not breaking when dropped and was able to stand slightly rougher treatment than wood. The inside was often pitched (covered with a resinous black substance) to make the container watertight.

You will need

Black leather, about $1/16$in thick

White paper for black and white photocopying

Darning needle

Medium-grade sandpaper

24-gauge paper-covered wire, $3^1/2$in length

Black acrylic paint

Black and dark brown shoe polish

Tacky glue

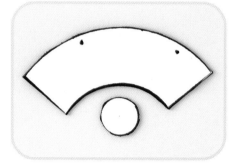

1 Photocopy and cut out the two leather bucket templates on page 61. Place the templates on the underside of the leather and cut to shape using sharp scissors. Use a darning needle to pierce through the leather where indicated on the larger template.

2 Take the body of the bucket and use a craft knife to remove thin slivers on the underside of the leather at one end, approximately $1/8$in wide. Turn the leather over and repeat the procedure on the top side of the leather at the other end.

Variation

Make a mug using the same instructions and the three mug templates on page 61. Remove thin slivers of leather on the underside of the handle at each end and then position and glue the handle on to the outside of the mug.

3 Rub sandpaper over the leather pieces to remove the shine. Rub a small amount of black and brown shoe polish around the edges and over each side to age, but do not buff. Paint the paper-covered wire black and when dry rub over with black shoe polish.

4 Glue the two side edges of the bucket together, so the top of the leather overlaps the underside. Once dry, position and glue the circular base inside the bucket. Poke each end of the wire through the outside holes, forming a loop at each end.

17

Box-seat Settle

During Tudor times, chairs were reserved for the head of the household. The design for this miniature version of a box-seat settle is thought to have originated from a chest placed against a wall and used as a seat. Panelled backs were often high to exclude draughts. This settle features a storage area under a sliding seat panel.

You will need

$^1/_8$in thick obechi sheet wood, $1^5/_8$in x $1^1/_4$in for base

$^3/_{32}$in thick obechi sheet wood:
    two $1^3/_8$in x $^1/_4$in lengths for arm rests
    4in x $1^5/_8$in for seat back
    two $2^5/_8$in x $1^1/_8$in for sides
    $1^5/_8$in x $1^3/_8$in for front (grain to run with shortest length)
    $1^5/_8$in x $1^3/_8$in for seat

$^3/_{16}$in x $^3/_{16}$in obechi strip wood:
    two 4in lengths for back posts
    two $2^5/_8$in lengths for front posts

$^1/_4$in x $^1/_{16}$in obechi strip wood:
    five $1^5/_8$in lengths for horizontal back and front panels
    six $1^1/_8$in for side panels
    $^7/_8$in for vertical front panel
    $1^1/_4$in length for vertical back panel

$^1/_8$in x $^1/_{16}$in obechi strip wood, two $1^1/_8$in for seat supports

Two $^3/_{16}$in diameter wooden doorknobs

Oak-coloured shoe polish

Tacky glue

1 Take the two pieces of wood for the arm rests and place together. Use sandpaper to shape the pieces as shown on the template on page 62. Sand and colour all of the wood components using oak-coloured shoe polish (see Basic Techniques page 12).

2 Take the seat back wood piece and the two back posts and glue the posts on to each side edge of the sheet wood. The underside of the seat back and the posts should be flush with each other.

3 Take a horizontal back panel and position at the top of the construction, so the panel edge is flush with the top edge of the seat back. (Note, remaining back panels are positioned once the settle has been constructed.)

4 Take a side wood piece and a front post and glue the post on to one side edge of the sheet wood. The underside of the side wood piece and the post should be flush with each other.

5 Repeat the procedure described in step 4 with the remaining side wood piece and post, making this construction a mirror image of the previous one.

6 Take the side panels and position the first panels at the top of each construction. Leave a gap of $5/8$in before positioning the second horizontal panels. Position the third panels at the bottom of the constructions. Glue all the panels into place.

7 Turn the panelled sides over to face down, with the wider gap between the panels at the bottom of the structures. Mark $1\frac{1}{4}$in upwards from the bottom of each construction. Glue a seat support on the marked line on each side wood piece.

8 Take the front wood piece (grain to run with the shortest length) and position two horizontal front panels on top of the wood, as shown. Place the vertical front panel centrally between the horizontal panels and glue into place.

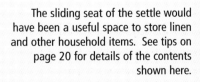

9 Position and glue the front construction between the two side constructions, with the front butting up to the end of the seat supports. Position the back construction so the inside edges of the back posts are in line with the side sheet wood pieces.

The sliding seat of the settle would have been a useful space to store linen and other household items. See tips on page 20 for details of the contents shown here.

19

Tip

You can create the pewter plates shown in the settle on page 19 by spraying $^{13}/_{16}$in diameter aluminium dinner plates with pewter enamel spray paint.

10 Take the base wood piece and glue it into the bottom of the box-seat settle so all outside edges are flush.

11 Slide the seat wood piece on to the settle. Glue a horizontal back panel on to the back immediately above the seat, allowing for the removal of the seat. Position and glue the remaining vertical back panel and horizontal back panel as shown, together with the arm rests.

12 Use a $^{1}/_{16}$in drill bit to drill a hole centrally into the top of each back post. Glue the wooden doorknobs into place, as shown in the main photograph on page 18.

Variation

This rustic version of the box-seat settle has been painted and distressed following the instructions on page 12. It too could be filled with linen and plates – see page 36 for how to make patterned country-style plates.

Tip

Fill the settle with folded pieces of fine wool cloth and cotton to imitate bedding.

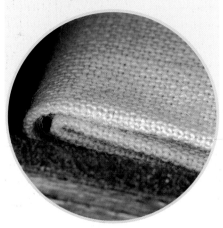

Classical Style

Console Table

Console tables were introduced into Britain from France during the 18th century, the word console meaning bracket in French. The principle characteristic of a console table is that it has two legs at the front, while the back is supported by a wall bracket. Pier tables are similar and stand against a wall between two windows, often with a matching mirror above.

You will need

$\frac{1}{16}$in thick obechi sheet wood, $2\frac{1}{2}$in x $1\frac{1}{4}$in

$\frac{1}{4}$in x $\frac{1}{8}$in obechi strip wood:
  $2\frac{3}{4}$in length for front
  two $1\frac{1}{4}$in lengths for sides

Filigree decorations

22-gauge florist's stub wire, two $2\frac{1}{4}$in lengths

Four 25mm x 4mm gold-plated fluted tube beads

Four 4mm diameter round gold-plated beads

Cream spray paint

Gold metallic paste

Marble-effect card, $2^{13}/_{16}$in x $1^{7}/_{16}$in

Tacky glue

Superglue gel

Tip

To give a sheen to the marble-effect card, ensure that it is securely stuck to the table-top before covering it with a 3-D gloss varnish (see page 9).

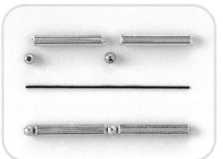

1 Take the wood pieces for the front and sides and glue them to the outside edges of the obechi sheet wood piece as shown. Once dry, use fine-grade sandpaper to sand the edges smooth and to slightly round the two corners at the front of the table.

2 Position and glue the filigree decorations symmetrically to the front and sides of the table-top using tacky glue. It may be necessary to glue each side separately, allowing each to dry before continuing with the next. Cut the filigrees with small pliers to ensure a good fit.

3 To make the legs, take a length of florist's stub wire and thread on two tube beads and two round beads, using superglue gel to fix into place. Repeat with the remaining wire and beads. Spray the table-top and legs with cream spray paint and leave to dry.

4 Rub over the table-top and legs with gold paste to highlight the filigrees and accentuate the fluted legs. Before gluing the marble-effect card on the top, round the corners slightly on one long side, in line with the table-top. Superglue the legs into place.

Neo-classical Mirror

Neo-classicism appeared in Europe during the middle of the 18th century and is often associated with Robert Adam (1728–92) who established his own distinctive style of decoration and ornamentation during that time. Mirrors were mostly gilded or painted cream and elegantly carved or decorated with gesso or plaster. Sconces were often attached to the frames so the mirror reflected the light from the candles into the room.

You will need

$^3/_{16}$in x $^1/_{16}$in obechi strip wood:
  two 2$^1/_4$in lengths
  two 2in lengths

$^1/_8$in x $^1/_{16}$in obechi strip wood:
  two 2$^1/_4$in lengths
  two 2in lengths

Plastic mirror, 2in x 1$^3/_4$in

Three gold-plated filigree strips

Three tiny gold-plated filigree flowers

Two gold-plated spokes

Two 3mm brass eyelets

Two slim white cake candles

Cream spray paint

Gold metallic paste

Tacky glue

Superglue gel

Variation

Revivals of the neo-classical style make this type of mirror suitable, more or less, up to the beginning of the 20th century. Frames can be decorated using a variety of filigrees and jewellery findings. Spray with old gold spray paint to achieve the effect of gilt wood.

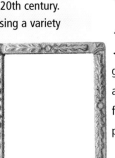

1 Take the four lengths of $^3/_{16}$in x $^1/_{16}$in strip wood and mitre the ends of each to an angle of 45 degrees (see page 12). Position and glue the mitred wood strips together as shown. Repeat the procedure with the $^1/_8$in x $^1/_{16}$in strip wood pieces.

2 Position and glue the $^1/_8$in wide strip wood construction on top of the $^3/_{16}$in wide strip wood construction to make a frame for the mirror and leave to dry. Use fine-grade sandpaper to sand smooth the side edges and corners of the frame.

3 Place the frame with the $^3/_{16}$in wide strip wood facing upwards and position and glue the filigree decorations symmetrically around the frame, ensuring that space is left for the sconces. Cut the filigrees with small pliers if necessary to ensure a good fit.

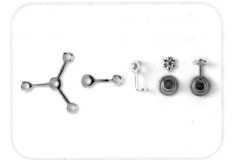

4 Remove two rods on each spoke and bend into an L shape. Superglue the sconce components together and on to the frame. Spray the frame with cream spray paint. Once dry, rub over with gold paste to highlight the filigrees. Glue mirror and candles into place.

Pedestals

Pedestals have been used for centuries to display a variety of items, such as busts, urns, candles and plants. Before the 18th century they were mostly made out of stone or wood but after this lighter materials such as papier mâché and plaster were often used. The basic principles of classical style were, and still are, symmetry and proportion, so therefore pedestals should be made and displayed in pairs, as detailed here.

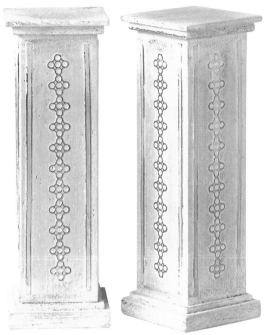

You will need

$^3/_{32}$in thick obechi sheet wood:
    four 3in x $^7/_8$in for wide sides
    four 3in x $^{11}/_{16}$in for narrow sides
    two 1in x 1in for lower tops

$^1/_{16}$in thick obechi sheet wood:
    two 1$^1/_8$in x 1$^1/_8$in for upper tops
    two 1in x 1in for upper bases

$^3/_{16}$in thick obechi sheet wood,
    two 1$^1/_8$in x 1$^1/_8$in for lower bases

One sheet of gold peel-off motifs
    containing borders and scrolls

One sheet of gold peel-off motifs
    containing straight borders

Antique white water-based
    acrylic paint

Gold metallic paste

Fine-grade wire wool

Tacky glue

Variation

Pedestals can be painted to represent various materials to suit home or garden from the 16th century onwards. The pedestal sides have been reduced to 2in and filigrees used as decoration. A plaster model was painted to match the stone-effect pedestal.

1 Use fine-grade sandpaper to sand the edges of all of the wooden components. Position and glue two narrow sides between two wide sides, so that all outside edges are flush with each other. Repeat this procedure for the second pedestal.

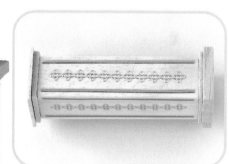

3 Position and glue the glued-wood sections centrally to each end of the column. Repeat for the second pedestal. Remove the peel-off stickers from the sheets and position on each side of the pedestals, ensuring the straight borders cover the joints.

2 Take the lower top wood pieces and glue centrally to the upper top wood pieces, with the grains of each wood piece running in opposite directions to each other to prevent warping. Repeat the procedure with the lower base and upper base wood pieces.

4 Paint the pedestals with antique white acrylic paint and leave to dry. Rub a small amount of gold metallic paste lightly over each pedestal. Add character and depth by gently rubbing with wire wool to give a sheen and highlight the decorative motifs.

Ornamental Mask

A traditional feature of neo-classical interior design is the display of classical Roman and Greek antiquities. Reproductions of statues and busts, often carved out of stone or moulded from plaster and decorated, became the vogue. This ornamental mask is made from a mould using polymer clay which is then decorated to create the effect of stone. Moulds suitable for making one-twelfth scale dolls' house dolls can be purchased through craft shops or from sugar-craft (cake-decorating) suppliers.

You will need

Face mould

Polymer clay

Talcum powder

Stone-effect paint (or grey and cream acrylic water-based paint, mixed with a little sand and tacky glue)

$\frac{1}{8}$in thick obechi sheet wood, $\frac{1}{2}$in x $\frac{1}{2}$in

Cocktail stick

Tacky glue

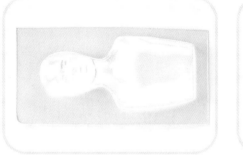

1 The mould shown here is from a set of body sugar-craft moulds. Before using the mould dust it with talcum powder each time.

2 Roll a ball of polymer clay to the required size and shape it into a teardrop as shown. Point the narrow end into the nose of the mould, pressing and smoothing the back as shown.

Variation

Sculptures made out of plaster and resin are available from egg-decorating suppliers and can be decorated in many ways depending upon your dolls' house needs. See pedestal, left.

3 Ease the clay gently out of the mould and trim the neck. Harden the clay by baking in a domestic oven following the manufacturer's instructions. Once cool, use a $\frac{1}{16}$in drill bit and drill a hole up through the neck.

4 Make a stand by drilling a $\frac{1}{16}$in hole through the centre of the piece of obechi wood. Join the head and base using a short length of cocktail stick. Paint with stone-effect paint or with cream and grey acrylic paint mixed with a little sand and tacky glue.

Neo-classical Vase

Neo-classicism was stimulated by the findings from archaeological excavations of the classical ruins at Herculaneum and Pompeii in Italy during the mid 18th century. Reproductions of ancient Greek and Roman stoneware were made to complement the neo-classical style of interior design and furnishing so popular during the mid-Georgian era. It would be useful to read the tip below before beginning this project.

You will need

Packet of 3mm width quilling paper

Quilling tool

Stone-effect paint (or grey and cream acrylic water-based paint, mixed with a little sand and tacky glue)

Tacky glue

1 Take a strip of quilling paper and place one end into the slot at the top of the quilling tool and begin to twist the handle. At the same time wind the paper tightly and neatly around the top of the tool until the whole strip has been coiled. Secure the ends with a dab of glue.

2 Take another strip of quilling paper and dab glue on to one end. Place on the coil so the glued area overlaps the previous end and continue to wind around in the same way. Remove from the quilling tool and repeat the procedure, using your fingers, until the paper coil measures $^3/_4$in diameter.

Tip

It is advisable to practise making small single bowls and vases before attempting the larger vase. Follow the steps, first coiling paper to measure approximately $^1/_2$in diameter and using the end of a pencil to press and ease it into shape. Paint your bowls and vases according to your requirements.

3 Following the previous steps make another paper coil to measure 1$^1/_8$in diameter. Taking one of the coils, use your fingers to *gently and carefully* press and ease the paper outwards to form a bowl shape. Repeat with the remaining paper coil.

4 Paint the bowls and fill the holes inside and out with diluted tacky glue and leave to dry. Position the larger bowl on top of the upturned smaller bowl and glue into position. Paint with stone-effect paint or with a paint, sand and glue mixture.

Topiary Trees

Topiary, the art of cutting trees, bushes and hedges into ornamental shapes, dates back to ancient times. Topiary trees cut into shapes such as balls, cones and pyramids became particularly fashionable during the 17th century because of their symmetrical profile. It was the Victorians, however, who developed topiary and created more unusual irregular shapes such as animals.

You will need

Four cocktail sticks

Two 1in egg-shaped paper balls

Green scenic scatter material

Two 1in high terracotta plant pots

5mm width decorative braid,
   8in length

Water-based acrylic paint

Gold metallic paste

Dry tea leaves

Tacky glue

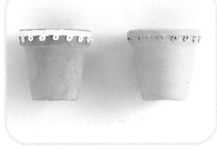

1 Paint two cocktail sticks with brown acrylic paint to represent a tree trunk. Use the remaining cocktail sticks to temporarily hold the paper balls and paint with green acrylic paint. Once dry, cover the balls with diluted tacky glue, dip them into the scatter material and leave to dry. If the scatter coverage is insufficient repeat the procedure after the glue has totally dried.

2 Position and glue the decorative braid around the top of each plant pot. Paint with acrylic paint and once dry rub over with gold paste. Mix dry tea leaves with tacky glue and press into each pot for soil. Place a painted cocktail stick into each ball and 'plant' before the soil mixture dries.

Variation

Paper balls are available in a variety of sizes and shapes. The triple-ball topiary tree has a hole through the two largest balls so once they have been covered with the scatter material they can be threaded on to a length of painted $3/32$in wood dowel.

Tip

When making topiary, unvarnished wooden beads may be used to create the rounded shapes instead of paper balls, as in the tree, far right.

Silhouettes

Silhouettes were a consequence of the neo-classical revival during the 18th century. The interior designs of Robert Adam favoured classical profiles and it was during this time that silhouette art was at its peak, coupled with the fact that other methods of capturing a person's likeness were expensive and time consuming. Miniature silhouettes were either painted or cut out of black paper and mounted.

You will need

Gold-plated oval pendant frame,
$^5/_{16}$in x $^3/_8$in

Black enamel spray paint

White paper for photocopying

Tacky glue

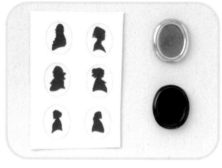

1 Spray the front of the frame with black enamel spray paint. Colour photocopy the small oval-bordered silhouette templates on page 61 on to white paper.

2 Use small, sharp scissors to cut around the border of a silhouette. Rub a small amount of tacky glue on to the underside, then position and glue the silhouette in the centre of the black oval frame.

Variation

By the late 18th and early 19th centuries the vogue for having a profile captured meant that many portrait artists were able to supplement their income by painting inexpensive silhouettes of each family member. These were often displayed in groups or hung on a ribbon. Make several framed silhouettes, as above, and glue them on to 2mm wide silk ribbon, topped with a bow (see page 54 for making bows).

Variation

Silhouettes can be given a different appearance by being enlarged and aged. Photocopy the larger oval silhouette templates on page 61, as described in step 1 above, and then age the silhouette by rubbing a very light brown shoe polish over the paper. A coat of 3-D gloss varnish (see page 9) at the end of step 2 will give the effect of a glass cover.

Tip

To antique a metal frame, spray the front with black enamel spray paint. Once dry, rub the smallest amount of gold paste over the frame to highlight any raised areas.

Country Style

Side Table

Side tables originated during the 15th century and were designed to stand against a wall. However, it wasn't until the 18th century that they became fashionable (see also the console table, page 22). The side table was used as an additional surface in the dining room at mealtimes, a display table in the drawing room and a place to leave your calling card in hallways of well-to-do homes. This table has been painted and distressed to achieve the 'look' so often associated with country style.

You will need

$^1/_{16}$in thick obechi sheet wood,
  2$^3/_8$in x 1$^3/_{16}$in for table-top

$^1/_4$in x $^1/_8$in obechi strip wood:
  two 2in lengths for long table-top
    supports
  two $^7/_8$in for short table-top supports

$^1/_8$in x $^1/_8$in obechi strip wood:
  four 2$^1/_8$in for legs
  2in length for long leg support
  two $^7/_8$in for short leg supports

Water-based acrylic paint

Water-based wood stain

Tacky glue

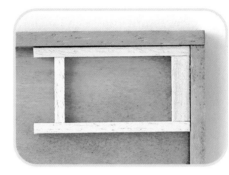

1 Sand each of the individual wooden components. Place two legs, a short table-top support and a short leg support (positioned $^1/_4$in from the end of each leg) in a right-angled gluing jig (see page 8) and glue together. Repeat the procedure with the remaining two legs and short supports.

2 Once dry, take the leg constructions and place downwards in a gluing jig. Position the long table-top supports between the leg structures and glue into place. Glue the long leg support centrally between the two short leg supports.

Variation

This side table was shoe polished before construction, with a false drawer and shelf added to the basic structure. Use the template on page 62 to cut out two wood pieces from $^1/_{16}$in thick obechi sheet wood. Position and glue one piece under the table-top supports and the other on top of the leg supports. Glue two wooden drawer knobs to the front of the false drawer to complete the look.

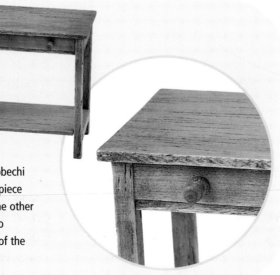

3 Glue the table-top in position so that at the back the side edge is flush with the leg structure, while the remaining side edges and front overhang by $^1/_{16}$in. Paint the table using water-based acrylic paints (see page 12 for distressing technique).

Side Chair

Back stools, literally a stool with a back, evolved at the beginning of the 17th century. They were used primarily in upper class homes at mealtimes, and when not in use they would line the walls of the room. By the beginning of the 18th century, full and elaborate sets of armless side chairs were being made for dining rooms and reception halls. Country-style versions were less ornate and often painted.

You will need

$\frac{1}{8}$in x $\frac{1}{8}$in obechi strip wood:
  two 2$\frac{7}{8}$in lengths for back leg
  two 1$\frac{3}{8}$in lengths for front legs
  six 1in lengths for slats

$\frac{1}{4}$in x $\frac{1}{8}$in obechi strip wood,
  four 1in lengths for seat supports

$\frac{1}{16}$in thick obechi sheet wood,
  1$\frac{1}{4}$in x 1$\frac{1}{4}$in for seat

Water-based acrylic paints

Water-based wood stain

Tacky glue

Variation

Since its introduction in the 1660s cane-seated furniture has been popular due to the lightness, durability and elasticity of cane. This seat is made using the instructions above but substituting the seat wood for a 1$\frac{3}{16}$in square piece of brown tapestry canvas (18 holes to the inch). Remove a $\frac{3}{32}$in square from the corners on one side and glue on to the seat frame.

1 Sand each of the wooden components. Position a slat and a seat support between two front legs, place into a right-angled gluing jig (see page 8) and glue into position, referring to the template on page 62.

2 Position three slats and a seat support between two back legs, place into the gluing jig and glue into position, referring to the template on page 62.

3 Turn the back and front constructions on their sides and place into the jig. Position and glue a slat and seat support between the leg structures and in line with the other supports. Repeat the procedure on the opposite side of the chair.

4 Take the seat piece and mark $\frac{1}{8}$in square out of the corners on a side that has the grain running along. Remove the two sections, first cutting against the grain to avoid splitting. Glue the seat on the frame and once dry see page 12 for paint distressing.

31

Wall Shelves

Developments in the production of books at the beginning of the 19th century increased the popularity of reading; previously it had been an occupation of only the very wealthy. Small sets of open shelves suitable for displaying and storing books, together with china and other ornaments, became a popular wall accessory.

You will need

$1/2$in x $1/16$in obechi strip wood, two $1 5/8$in lengths for sides

$7/16$in x $1/16$in obechi strip wood, two $2 1/2$in lengths for shelves

$1/8$in x $1/16$in obechi strip wood, two $1 5/8$in for back supports

$3/8$in diameter hardwood dowel

Light brown wood stain

Tacky glue

Variation

This is a slightly more elaborate set of polished wall shelves. Follow step 1 above and then place the shelf sides together and mark $9/16$in from the straight end. Sand and shape the wood at the marked point using the dowel and sandpaper tool. Colour the wooden components with brown shoe polish, buffing to a sheen with wire wool before assembling.

1 Take a back support wood piece and mark $1/8$in along from one corner of the wood. Join the mark to the corner opposite and remove the triangular section. Use fine-grade sandpaper to gently sand the wood smooth. Repeat the procedure with the other back support.

2 Take the side wood pieces and mark $5/16$in along from one corner on each and remove the triangular sections. Wind a piece of fine-grade sandpaper around the piece of dowel, place the two side wood pieces together and sand and shape the cut sections of the wood as shown.

3 Position the side wood pieces to be a mirror image of each other. From the straight end on each, mark across at $1/8$in and then 1in. Sand the remaining wooden components using fine-grade sandpaper and then stain with a light brown wood stain.

4 Position and glue the back supports on top of the side wood pieces as shown, keeping all side edges flush. Take the two shelf wood pieces and position and glue the ends of each in line with the pencil marks on the shelf sides.

Books

Towards the end of the Victorian era, advances in printing techniques and processes meant that books became available to a mass market. Here we are creating the effect of a pile or row of books for the country-style wall shelves described opposite. Even though each book is created individually, they are not made with fine detail, that is, with separate pages and a printed front cover, as it would take forever to fill the shelves!

You will need

$\frac{1}{2}$in x $\frac{3}{32}$in obechi strip wood, 4in length

$\frac{3}{8}$in x $\frac{3}{32}$in obechi strip wood, 3in length

$\frac{1}{2}$in x $\frac{1}{16}$in obechi strip wood, 4in length

$\frac{3}{8}$in x $\frac{1}{16}$in obechi strip wood, 3in length

Selection of coloured pastel paper

Water-based acrylic paint

Brown and black shoe polish

Gold metallic paste

Tacky glue

Book sizes

Follow the guide below to make different sized books:

$\frac{1}{2}$in x $\frac{3}{32}$in obechi strip – $\frac{5}{8}$in spine length;

$\frac{3}{8}$in x $\frac{3}{32}$in obechi strip – $\frac{1}{2}$in spine length;

$\frac{1}{2}$in x $\frac{1}{16}$in obechi strip – $\frac{3}{4}$in spine length;

$\frac{3}{8}$in x $\frac{1}{16}$in obechi strip – $\frac{7}{16}$in spine length.

1 Take the $\frac{1}{2}$in x $\frac{3}{32}$in strip of wood and use fine-grade sandpaper to gently round one long side edge, to create the effect of the book spine. Cut the strip into $\frac{5}{8}$in lengths using either a mitre block and saw or mitre cutters. Sand any rough edges.

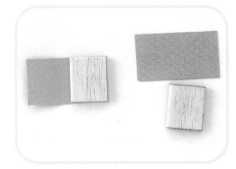

2 Cut out a book cover from the pastel paper and rub the outside of the paper with a small amount of shoe polish or gold metallic paste to age it. Rub paste or shoe polish along the straight outside edges of a wooden block to create the effect of the pages.

3 Rub a thin, even layer of tacky glue on the inside of the book cover and glue on to the block of wood. Use the blunt edge of a knife to make horizontal indentations on the spine of the book. Make more books using the remaining strip wood – see guide, left.

4 As an alternative to making paper book covers, paint some wooden blocks using water-based acrylic paints. Age the painted cover by lightly rubbing over shoe polish or gold paste. Position the painted books between paper-covered books for best results.

Log Basket

Basket making is an ancient craft and the principles of making and weaving baskets out of natural materials has altered little since primitive times. For many centuries wicker baskets, with their lightness and durability, have been an invaluable means of storing and transporting goods. Developments in technology during the 20th century have caused a decline in the use of wicker baskets.

You will need

24-gauge white paper-covered floral wire:
    nine 7in lengths for stakes
    two 1$\frac{1}{2}$in lengths for handles
    two 1in lengths for inside handles

Brown waxed thread, 15m (16yd)

Medium oak water-based wood stain

Cocktail stick

Tacky glue

Dried twigs for logs

Tip
Use mitre cutters or a saw and mitre block (shown on page 12) to cut dried twigs to fill your basket with miniature logs.

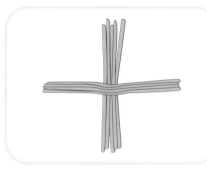

1 Stain all of the paper-covered wire with medium oak wood stain and leave to dry. Lay four stakes centrally on top of the remaining five stakes as shown above.

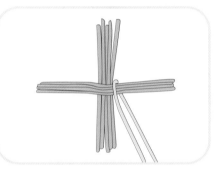

2 Take the waxed thread and fold over a 5in length to form a loop. Begin to secure the stakes together by placing the loop around one group of stakes as shown above.

3 Take the thread that is under the first group of stakes, over the top of the second group of stakes. The thread that is over the first group should be brought under the second group of stakes.

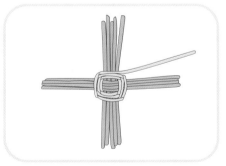

4 Continue this under-and-over pattern neatly and evenly around the groups of stakes in three full circles. Trim the short excess length of weaving thread, dabbing on a tiny amount of tacky glue to hold it in place.

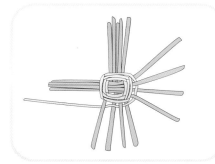

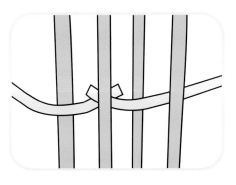

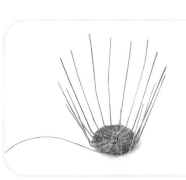

5 Cut off one stake with wire cutters to leave seventeen – an uneven number is needed to weave alternately in and out of each stake. Begin to weave between the stakes, opening them out as you do so.

If you come to the end of the thread whilst weaving, join a new length behind a stake on the inside of the basket, as above.

6 Ensure the stakes remain evenly spaced during weaving and the weaving thread kept tight and even. Continue weaving until the base measures $1\frac{1}{8}$in diameter, then begin to bend the stakes upwards and outwards slightly.

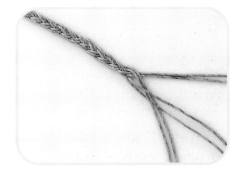

7 Continue weaving until the basket is $1\frac{1}{8}$in high, ensuring the stakes remain slightly angled outwards. When the weaving is finished, use the end of cocktail stick to dab a tiny amount of tacky glue around the top of the basket next to the stakes.

8 Once the glue has dried, trim the stakes to the height of the woven thread using wire cutters. Trim the excess weaving thread and dab a tiny amount of tacky glue on the end to hold it in place inside the basket.

9 To make the border for the top of the basket, take six 12in lengths of waxed thread and using two together, plait into a length. Trim each end and glue on to the top of the basket to hide the ends of the wire stakes.

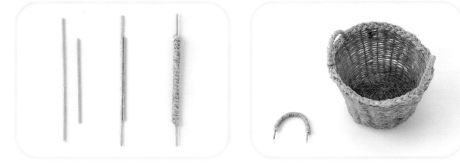

10 To make a handle, take a $1\frac{1}{2}$in and 1in length of wire. Place together and neatly wind around the waxed thread, leaving a $\frac{1}{4}$in gap at each end of the wire. Use tacky glue to secure the thread at each end. Repeat with the remaining handle wires.

11 Bend the handles into shape, then take a handle and glue each wire end in through the border and between the weaving. Repeat with the remaining handle on the opposite side. Chop twigs into small lengths and use to fill up the log basket.

Variation
This shopping basket has been made in the same way as the log basket. Stain nine $4\frac{1}{2}$in lengths (stakes), one $2\frac{1}{4}$in length and one $1\frac{3}{4}$in length (handle) of paper-covered wire with antique pine stain and use ecru and brown waxed thread for weaving. Weave the base until it measures 1in diameter, then bend the stakes upwards and continue weaving until the basket is $\frac{5}{8}$in high.

Plates

Advances in technology due to the industrial revolution resulted in good quality, decorative ceramics being mass produced at a much more affordable price than imported or hand-painted ceramics. Ribbon plates were not made until the end of the 19th century, although the piercing of plates dates back to the 15th century.

You will need

For the plates:

$^{13}/_{16}$in diameter aluminium dinner plates

Water-slide transfers (decals)

White or cream enamel spray paints

Tacky glue

For the ribbon plates:

$^{13}/_{16}$in diameter paper dinner plates

Water-slide transfers (decals)

White or cream enamel spray paints

$^{1}/_{16}$in diameter circle paper punch

2mm width silk ribbon

Needle

Tacky glue

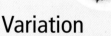

Variation

Two 1in diameter aluminium dinner plates have been decorated following the same basic instructions. To achieve the shiny appearance the plates have been given a coat of 3-D gloss varnish (see page 9).

Plates

1 Spray an aluminium plate front and back with enamel spray paint. Trim excess paper from around the transfer and then soak in a dish of water for several minutes until the transfer separates from the paper backing.

Ribbon Plates

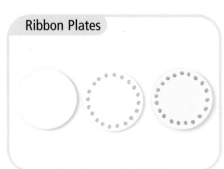

1 Take a paper plate and use a $^{1}/_{16}$in paper punch to pierce an even number of holes around the border. The plate shown here has twenty holes, with a gap of approximately $^{1}/_{16}$in between each. Paint the front and back of the plate with enamel spray paint.

2 Rub a small amount of tacky glue over the middle of the plate and place the transfer centrally on the plate, smoothing out any air bubbles. Once dry, cover the plate with diluted tacky glue to cover and conceal the edge of the transfer.

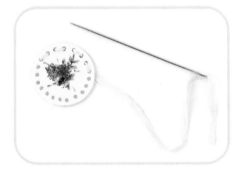

2 Follow the instructions in steps 1 and 2 from the basic plate above to apply and cover the transfer. Thread the ribbon in and out of the holes on the plate using a needle. Trim each end of the ribbon and glue to the back of the plate.

Candlesticks and Snuffer

Candles have been used in Britain since Roman times and until the end of 19th century were the most common form of artificial lighting (see also the torchère on page 15). All levels of society have used candlesticks and more have been made out of brass than any other material. The small, hollow, cone-shaped snuffer is used to extinguish a burning candle.

You will need

Two 3mm brass eyelets

Two gold-plated spacer beads,
   6mm x 3mm

Slim white cake candle

Gold-plated bell cap

Gold-plated head pin

Black water-based acrylic paint

Superglue gel

1 Take a brass eyelet and place it wide side down. Insert a gold-plated spacer bead into the upturned opening of the eyelet using superglue gel to secure it. Repeat the procedure for the second candlestick.

2 Take the candle and cut two $^3/_4$in lengths. To avoid the wax fracturing, roll the candle backwards and forwards whilst using a craft knife to slice through the wax and cut the wick. Remove $^1/_8$in of wax on each candle to reveal the wick and then insert into the holders.

Variation

Make Christmas candlesticks following the same instructions but using red or green cake candles. Make a collar for each out of a tinsel pipe cleaner, slot this on to the candlestick and rest it on the foot ring.

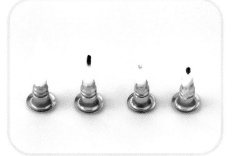

3 To achieve the effect of burnt candles, light the candles and let them burn part of the way down. Cut the wick down to size, as it will not have burnt as quickly as the wax, then colour the wick with black water-based acrylic paint.

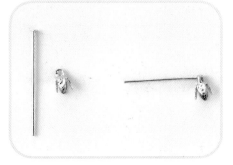

4 To make the snuffer, take the gold-plated bell cap and head pin. Cut the head pin to measure $^3/_4$in long and slide the eye of the bell cap along to the end of the head pin, gluing into place with superglue gel.

Decoy Duck

Hunters have used carved wooden ducks for centuries as decoys to lure wildfowl within range of their weapons. The decoy ducks were often painted to bring them to life and then weighted to float on water, as flocks of wildfowl will often join other resting and seemingly secure birds in the water. Decoy ducks can be decorative and are often associated with American folk art.

You will need

Cold porcelain modelling paste (see page 10)

22-gauge florist's stub wire, painted black

$\frac{1}{8}$in thick obechi sheet wood, $\frac{1}{4}$in x $\frac{1}{4}$in

Medium oak water-based wood stain

Black and cream water-based acrylic paints

Black enamel paint

Tacky glue

1 Take the cold porcelain modelling paste and roll out a $\frac{3}{8}$in diameter ball. Simply shape the ball into the body of a duck. Roll out a $\frac{1}{4}$in diameter ball for the head and a $\frac{1}{16}$in ball and shape into a beak.

2 Attach the head and beak to the duck's body using a dab of tacky glue. Cut the stub wire to measure 1in long and insert into the base of the duck. Place the opposite end of the wire into a temporary holder, such as florist's foam, until the duck is dry and firm.

Variation

A stick-up is a flat-shaped panel supported on a stake and situated in fields as a decoy. Make this variation by transferring the duck template on page 62 on to a piece of thin brown card. Paint with black acrylic paint and lightly sand the edges. Make a stand following step 4, right, and glue the wire to the back of the duck.

3 Cover the duck with a light coat of medium oak wood stain. Once dry, lightly cover the top of the head, body and beak with black acrylic paint. Use a fine paintbrush to stroke cream paint over side of the face and breast. Use black enamel for the eyes.

4 To make the stand, drill a $\frac{3}{64}$in hole in the centre of the wooden block. Sand the block and then paint with black acrylic paint. Follow the paint distressing instructions on page 12 to age and add character to the stand. To finish, glue the wire into the wooden block.

Victorian Values

Hat and Coat Rack

Hooks and racks for hanging up coats and hats were to be found in entrance halls of many middle class homes during the Victorian and Edwardian eras. Large hallways would have been furnished with a hall stand, a functional piece of furniture used to deposit hats, coats, boots, umbrellas and walking sticks. This rack is ideal for a more confined space.

You will need

³⁄₃₂in obechi thick sheet wood, two 1in x 1in for sides

³⁄₈in x ¹⁄₈in obechi strip wood, 2¹⁄₂in length for hook support

¹⁄₈in x ¹⁄₁₆in obechi strip wood:
2¹⁄₂in length for back support
five 2⁷⁄₈in lengths for slats

Three 14mm wooden belaying pins for hooks

Dark wood stain or shoe polish

Tacky glue

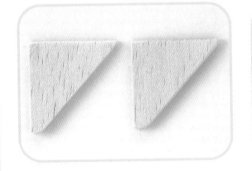

1 Transfer the coat and hat rack side template on page 62 on to the two pieces of sheet wood and use mitre cutters or a craft knife to remove excess wood. Sand the edges smooth using fine-grade sandpaper. Sand the strip wood pieces too.

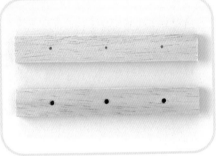

2 Take the hook support and transfer the drill hole positions from the template on page 62 on to the wood piece. Use a ¹⁄₁₆in drill bit to drill the holes part-way through the wood. Use a dark-coloured wood stain or shoe polish on all of the wooden components.

Variation

These simple racks of hooks are suitable from the Victorian era and onwards. Take a 2in length of ³⁄₈in x ¹⁄₈in obechi strip wood and transfer the drill hole positions on page 62. Follow steps 2 and 3, using four 14mm wooden belaying pins.

3 Remove part of the straight section of wood from the belaying pins using mitre cutters, leaving ¹⁄₁₆in attached to the turned head. Glue the straight ends of the belaying pins into the holes on the hook support.

4 Position and glue the hook support and back support between the two sides and leave to dry. Referring to the main photograph at the top of the page, glue two slats on top of the rack, in line with the back and front, and the other three slats in between.

Boater

Popular during the Victorian and Edwardian eras, this simply made boater is a decorative addition to the coat and hat rack opposite. Although traditionally made from straw, this gentleman's boater is made out of canvas. This method can be used to make a wide variety of hats by simply altering the size and shape of the hat block and brim. Felt or leather may be used as alternative materials.

You will need

Canvas (suit interlining)

Hat block (see step 1)

Small elastic band

3mm width black silk ribbon

Tacky glue

1 The crown of the boater is made by moulding the canvas over a hat block, such as a bottle top or wooden dowel measuring approximately $^3/_4$in diameter. Cut a piece of canvas $2^1/_2$in x $2^1/_2$in and soak in warm water for a minute.

2 Place the soaked canvas around the top of the mould and hold in place with a small elastic band. Manipulate the material until the canvas on top of the mould is flat and the outside, above the elastic band, is smooth. Once totally dry, remove and trim to measure $^1/_4$in high.

Variation

This hat has been made using a dome-shaped hat block and increasing the size of the brim to $1^5/_8$in. Shape the brim by dampening slightly and holding in shape until dry. Further decoration may be added to this hat, although if finely adorned it would have been stored in a hat box rather than on a hat rack.

3 Cover a $1^1/_2$in x $1^1/_2$in piece of canvas on one side with diluted tacky glue and leave to dry. Draw a $1^3/_8$in diameter circle on the glued side (underside) of the canvas, followed by a circle in the centre slightly smaller than the size of the crown and cut out.

4 Glue the crown on to the brim, with the glued side downwards. Trim the boater with a length of 3mm black silk ribbon. Make a bow as described on page 54, remove the ends and then flatten and glue it on, to cover the join in the ribbon band.

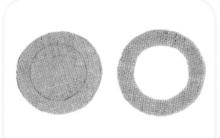

41

Stick Stand

During the Victorian and Edwardian eras, many entrance halls would have been furnished with a stick stand. Even though a stick stand was a practical piece of furniture, they were considered decorative when filled with the many walking sticks owned by the gentleman of the house. Mass production during the mid 19th century ensured that there were sticks available and affordable for a variety of occasions and purposes.

You will need

$^1/_{32}$in thick card, $1^3/_4$in x $^7/_8$in

$^1/_8$in x $^1/_8$in obechi strip wood:
   four $2^1/_2$in lengths for legs
   four $1^5/_8$in lengths for front and
      back supports
   six $^3/_4$in lengths for side and
      middle supports

$^1/_{32}$in thick obechi sheet wood,
   four $^3/_{16}$in x $^3/_{16}$in

Dark wood stain or shoe polish

Black and silver water-based
   acrylic paints

Tacky glue

1 Transfer the tray measurements from the template on page 62 on to the thick card and cut out. Paint the card with a mixture of black and silver acrylic paint to give the effect of a metallic tray base. Once dry, repeat the procedure on the other side of the card.

2 Sand and stain or shoe polish the wooden components. Take two legs and on each mark $^1/_8$in along from each end. Place into a right-angled gluing jig (see page 8) and position and glue two front supports between the legs, as shown. Repeat with the remaining legs and back supports.

Variation

Not all Victorian and Edwardian hallways were spacious, so you could make a smaller version of the stick stand by altering the measurements of the front and back supports to $^3/_4$in. See template on page 62 for the tray measurements.

3 Place the front and back sections into the gluing jig and glue the two side supports between, as shown. Once dry, position and glue two supports centrally into the stand and the remaining ones on to the opposite side.

4 Position and glue the tray underneath the stand. To complete, glue the squares of sheet wood on top of the legs.

Walking Sticks

For many centuries walking sticks (canes) have been considered a status symbol – the larger and more decorative the stick, the higher the rank or class of the owner. During the 19th century walking sticks were regarded as a fashionable accessory rather than an aid to walking, and it was unlikely a gentleman would have been seen out and about without one. Ebony walking sticks were a popular fashionable accessory for the evening.

You will need

$\frac{1}{16}$in diameter hardwood dowel, two 3in lengths

Aluminium foil, five pieces $\frac{5}{16}$in x $\frac{1}{16}$in

4mm round silver bead

4mm round black bead

Centre (reed) cane size 3, 5in length

Black enamel paint

Silver water-based acrylic paint

Wood stain or shoe polish

Tacky glue

Silver-topped Stick

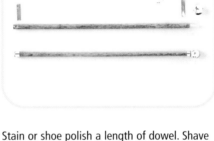

Stain or shoe polish a length of dowel. Shave one end and glue on a silver bead. Wind a length of aluminium foil around the shaft below the bead and glue in place for a collar. Repeat with another piece of foil to make a ferrule (tip) and glue into place. Touch up each end of the stick with silver acrylic paint.

Ebony Stick

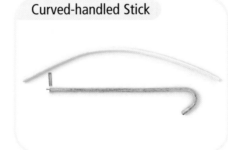

Take a length of dowel and paint with black enamel paint. Once dry, make a knob (using a black bead), collar and ferrule for the stick, as described left.

Curved-handled Stick

Stain a 5in length of size 3 centre cane. Soak in warm water for 20 minutes and then bend one end over a pencil. Hold in place with a clothes peg and straighten the opposite end. Once dry, trim the handle and stick to $3\frac{1}{8}$in. Make a ferrule, as described above.

Variation

Porcelain knobs on sticks were fashionable during the 19th century. Follow the instructions for the silver-topped stick but replace the silver bead with a porcelain or opaque glass bead. Wind 28-gauge wire immediately below the bead as an alternative collar. Gold foil is available from craft shops and can be used as an alternative to aluminium foil.

Plant Stand

The introduction of mass-produced furniture from about the 1850s onwards enabled many Victorians to fulfill their need to buy and accumulate decorative possessions for their homes. Not all furniture was made from quality wood but the Victorians were particularly good at imitating superior finishes on inferior-made items. This effective but simply made wooden plant stand is suitable to either the Victorian or Edwardian eras.

You will need

$^3/_{32}$in thick obechi sheet wood, two 1in x 1in

Round-ended spindle

Dark wood stain or shoe polish

Tacky glue

Variation

For a more contemporary look make a plant stand as described above but decorate it with a distressed paint finish in cream or a colour to complement your dolls' house décor (see page 12 for distressing technique instructions).

1 Take a wood piece and use a pencil and ruler to draw a line from corner to corner to find the centre. Measure and mark $^3/_{16}$in along from each corner then join the marks using a pencil and ruler.

2 Remove the corner sections using either mitre cutters or a craft knife. Chamfer the edges of the wood piece, on the side without the pencil marks, to an angle of 45 degrees using fine-grade sandpaper (see Basic Techniques page 12). Repeat steps 1 and 2 with the second piece of wood.

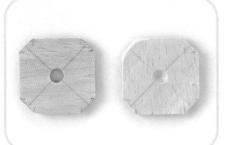

3 Measure the diameter of the wide end of your spindle and using the same sized drill bit, drill a hole centrally straight through a wood piece for the base. On the second piece, drill a hole the same size but only half-way through for the top.

4 Cut the narrow end off the spindle and sand smooth. Stain or shoe polish all the wooden components. Glue the straight end of the spindle into the base, chamfered side up. Glue the top into position, with the wood grain of both pieces in line with the base.

Aspidistra

The Victorians were passionate about gardening and were keen to bring the outdoors into their homes. Floral arrangements and plants would have graced many middle and upper class homes. The aspidistra was a popular houseplant as it was able to withstand many of the unsatisfactory living conditions of that time, such as draughts, fumes and shade. It became known as the 'cast-iron plant' because of its ability to survive in such circumstances.

You will need

Leaf green floral tape

26-gauge green paper-covered floral wire, twelve 2$\frac{1}{2}$in lengths

Dry tea leaves

Plant pot

Tacky glue

Variation

The spider plant (*Chlorophytum comosum*) has been a popular choice of houseplant for more than 200 years as it will grow in hot or cold rooms and sunny or shady corners. You will need light green floral tape and 33-gauge white paper-covered wire. Cut 30 lengths of tape 1$\frac{1}{2}$in to 4in. Follow step 1 and at the end of step 2 paint a fine line of antique white acrylic paint centrally along each side of the tape. Before the paint dries, run your finger along the line of the wire, to give a variegated effect to the leaf. Follow the remaining steps, using the template on page 61.

1 Cut twelve strips of floral tape into varying lengths ranging from 2$\frac{1}{2}$in to 1$\frac{1}{2}$in. Take a piece of floral tape and cover one half of the tape on one side with a thin layer of tacky glue. Place the wire centrally on the glued section of the tape, as shown.

2 Fold the tape over, so the wire is sandwiched between the tape. Press firmly, then slightly pull the end of the wire so the wire isn't right at the end of the fold. Repeat the procedure with the remaining materials and leave to dry.

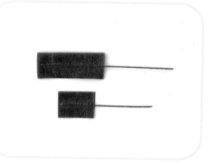

3 Transfer the leaf template from page 61 on to the longest floral tape pieces. Alter the length and width of the leaf accordingly and cut out the shapes. Trim the wire ends to 1in. Make soil by mixing dry tea leaves with tacky glue and press into your plant pot.

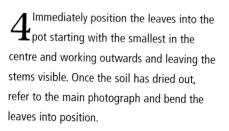

4 Immediately position the leaves into the pot starting with the smallest in the centre and working outwards and leaving the stems visible. Once the soil has dried out, refer to the main photograph and bend the leaves into position.

Framed Photographs

William Fox Talbot (1800–77) pioneered photography in the 1830s. During the Victorian and Edwardian eras, visits to the photographer's studio for formal family portraits were fashionable and often whole walls in the home were covered with framed photographs. By the end of the 19th century the simple box 'Brownie' and the Kodak camera allowed many people to take photographs themselves and amateur photography boomed.

You will need

White card for colour photocopying

Neutral-coloured paper for mounts

Paper punches:
- 1.5cm diameter circle,
- 1cm diameter circle,
- 1cm square,
- 1.3cm x 0.7cm rectangle

$1/8$in x $1/16$in jelutong strip wood

$3/32$in x $1/16$in jelutong strip wood

$1/16$in x $1/16$in jelutong strip wood

Wood stain

Tacky glue

1 Colour photocopy the sepia prints on page 61 on to white card. Use paper punches to punch holes out of the coloured paper to make a mount for each of the photographs, ensuring that the aperture is no larger than the photograph.

2 Cut out the photographs, leaving a small border around the outside. Cut the mounts to size, leaving no more than $1/4$in border around the aperture. Position and glue the photograph to the back of the mount.

3 Stain the lengths of strip wood and then make a frame for each photograph (see page 12). The frame should measure slightly larger than the outside edges of the mount. Alternatively, use moulded picture framing wood to frame the photographs.

Variation

Make small photograph frames out of metal frames used for egg decorating. They can be sprayed and antiqued (see tip on page 28), tarnished using wood stain or left in their natural state. Cut a photograph to fit and glue into position. Make a stand for the frame by folding a small strip of card into a V shape and gluing it to the back of the frame.

Trinkets

The Victorians loved accumulating ornamental accessories to display in their homes. Mass production from the 1850s onwards meant that mementoes and trinkets were available and affordable to many people. Collections of bric-a-brac would have been displayed on every available surface, whilst walls were cluttered with pictures and photographs.

You will need

Small selection of glass and ceramic beads, no larger than 1cm

Brass knobs,
   3mm and 2mm diameter

6mm diameter gold-plated decorative caps

10mm silver-plated up-eye

8mm gold-plated up-eye

6mm silver-plated up-eye

2mm silver-plated up-eye

8mm high gold-plated bead cap

3mm nickel eyelets

7mm high gold-plated bell

14mm wooden belaying pin

Enamel paints

Wood stain

Superglue gel

Variation

Dishes can be filled with 1mm diameter no-hole beads to represent bon-bons or with fragments of dried flowers to represent pot-pourri.

Bottles and Jars

Make decorative bottles and jars with glass and ceramic beads which have brass knobs or 2mm diameter up-eyes inserted. An interesting display of bottles can be made using a variety of different sized and shaped beads and up-eyes are also available gold plated.

Lidded Pots

Make lidded pots from glass and ceramic beads topped with 6mm gold-plated decorative caps. The relief pattern on some caps enables them to be enamelled. Dip a cocktail stick into enamel paint and allow a small droplet to fall into the area to be decorated.

Trinket Dishes

Make dishes from nickel eyelets with 10mm up-eyes inserted into the narrow end. Make a decorative pot using an 8mm diameter bead cap, topped with a 6mm up-eye. Make a trinket pot from an eyelet, capped with a 6mm up-eye.

Bells

Take the bell and remove the clapper using a small pair of pliers. Remove part of the straight section of the wood from a 14mm belaying pin, leaving $\frac{1}{8}$in attached to the turned head. Stain and then glue this into the top of the bell.

Bracket Lamps

Paraffin oil was discovered during the 1840s and within a few decades it had become available in large quantities and provided inexpensive and reliable lighting. Gas lighting was also popular although not all areas in Britain had supplies of gas. Wall fittings for oil lamps were known as bracket lamps and were commonly found in hallways and landings and often made to swing from side to side. The main components of these bracket lamps are findings used for egg decorating and they are for effect only and not for electrification.

You will need

$^1/_{16}$in diameter brass tube, two 1$^1/_4$in lengths

Two 5mm high gold-plated bells

Two 12mm diameter gold-plated up-eyes

Two frosted flower shades

$^3/_{16}$in diameter clear plastic tube, two $^1/_2$in lengths

Two gold-plated head pins

Superglue gel

Tacky glue

Variation

These glass oil burners (from the Victorian and Edwardian eras) are made from two 9mm pyramid glass beads and two $^3/_8$in lengths of cream button thread, which have been coloured at one end with black felt-tip pen and inserted into each bead.

1 Transfer the bracket lamp template on page 62 on to paper or card. Take a length of brass tube and with two pairs of small pliers, bend into the shape shown on the drawing. Repeat the procedure with the remaining piece of brass tube.

2 Use a small pair of pliers to remove the clappers from the bells. Check that the brass tube threads through the holes in the bells, the shades and the loop on each of the up-eyes. If you have difficulty, widen the holes carefully using a pin file.

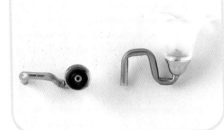

3 Thread the bell on to the brass tube, then position the shade on top of the upturned bell, so the end of the brass tube is just visible in the shade. Superglue into place, then repeat with the other lamp.

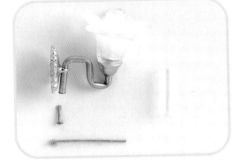

4 Use tacky glue to fix the clear plastic tube inside the base of the shade. Slide the brass tube on to the cap – do not glue, to enable the lamp to swing. Cut a head pin to $^1/_4$in and glue into the protruding end of the brass tube. Repeat for the second lamp.

Table Lamps

Practical and simple lamps were used to light functional rooms such as the kitchen, whilst in reception rooms like the parlour, lamps were ornamental and decorative. The oil lamp here is suitable for Victorian and Edwardian eras, whilst the mosaic glass Tiffany-style table lamp is appropriate from the end of 19th century up to the present day. Electrification is optional.

You will need

For the oil lamp:

8mm acrylic gold-plated corrugated ring bead

Gold-plated head pin

15mm acrylic gold-plated bead cap

25mm x 4mm gold-plated fluted tube bead

12mm x 6mm acrylic gold-plated cushion bead

Frosted flower shade

$3/16$in diameter clear plastic tube, $1/2$in length

12-volt grain-of-rice bulb with fine wires

Superglue gel

For the Tiffany lamp:

Gold-plated filigree shade

Black spray paint

Glass paints

Gold-plated spoke

25mm x 4mm gold-plated fluted tube bead

15mm acrylic gold-plated bead cap

5mm x 2mm brass washer bead

12-volt grain-of-wheat bulb with fine wires

Oil Lamp

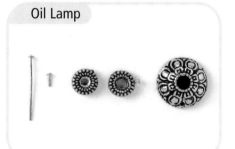

1 Use a $1/32$in drill bit to drill a hole part of the way through the side of the corrugated ring bead. Cut the head pin to measure $3/16$in and superglue the straight end into the drilled hole. Use a $1/16$in drill bit to drill a hole through the side of the bead cap, for electrification.

2 Glue the cap, tube and cushion beads together as shown, followed by the corrugated ring and shade. Thread the wires from the bulb down through the shade and out of the hole in the base. Rest the plastic tube in the shade, without gluing to allow replacement of the bulb.

Tiffany Lamp

1 Take the filigree shade and lightly spray inside and out with black spray paint. Take a cocktail stick, dip it into the glass paint and begin to fill the gaps in the shade symmetrically, allowing each colour to dry before continuing with the next.

2 Take the spoke and use pliers to slightly lift the loops at each end. Superglue the lamp stand together, following the oil lamp instructions for electrification details. Rest the shade on top of the upturned spokes – do not glue, to allow easy replacement of the bulb.

Papier Mâché Letter Rack

The technique of moulding paper pulp was introduced into Europe during the 17th century. Homeware and furniture made out of papier mâché became particularly fashionable during the Victorian era. Items were covered with japan, a hard, glossy black lacquer, originally from Japan and most commonly decorated with inlaid mother-of-pearl and floral paintings. This letter rack would have been used from the 1840s onwards following the introduction of the penny post, which made letter writing a popular pastime.

You will need

1/32in thickness card

1/16in diameter circle paper punch

Black water-based enamel paint

Water-slide transfers (decals) or acrylic water-based paints

Gold metallic paste

Tacky glue

Variation

Moulded papier mâché trays were a practical but decorative household item, popular in many Victorian homes. Trays can either be purchased and painted or sprayed with black enamel paint, or made out of card and decorated as described in step 4.

1 Transfer the letter rack templates on page 62 on to a piece of 1/32in thickness card. Use a sharp craft knife to score the card where indicated. Make a hole at the top of the rack using a 1/16in diameter paper punch.

2 Take the back piece of card and from the base, measure and mark with a pencil the following positions – 1/8in, 9/16in and 1in.

3 Take a letter holder and fold the sides down so the scored lines face outwards. Position and glue on to the back piece, so the base of the letter holder rests centrally on a marked line. Repeat the procedure with the remaining card pieces and leave to dry.

4 Paint the letter rack with black water-based enamel paint. Decorate the letter holders either by painting or using water-slide transfers soaked off and smoothed on to the front of each one. Highlight the outside edges of the back and holders with gold paste.

Edwardian
Christmas

Coal Box

Due to improvements in transport during the mid 19th century, coal became a cheap and reliable source of domestic fuel. Many homes had a fireplace in each room and fireside accessories were plentiful. This coal box is fitted with a small hook at the back of the box to hold a brass scoop. To avoid using hinges, which can be fiddly and expensive, the lid just slots on to the front of the box.

You will need

$\frac{1}{8}$in thick obechi sheet wood:
  $1\frac{3}{8}$in x $1\frac{1}{8}$in for base
  $1\frac{1}{8}$in x $\frac{7}{8}$in for back

$\frac{1}{16}$in thick obechi sheet wood:
  two $1\frac{1}{8}$in x $\frac{15}{16}$in for
    front and top
  two $1\frac{1}{2}$in x $1\frac{1}{16}$in for sides

$\frac{1}{16}$in x $\frac{1}{16}$in obechi strip wood:
  $1\frac{1}{8}$in length for front support
  two $\frac{3}{8}$in lengths for top supports

Wooden double column or small
  wooden drawer knob

Brass handle

Two brass pins, $\frac{1}{8}$in length

Gold-plated eye pin

Thin brass sheet, $\frac{7}{8}$in x $\frac{3}{8}$in

20-gauge brass wire, $\frac{3}{4}$in length

14mm wooden belaying pin

Model railway coal

Dark brown shoe polish

Black water-based acrylic paint

Tacky glue

Superglue gel

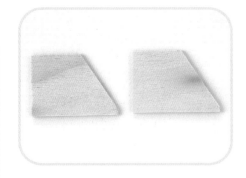

1 Transfer the coal box side template (page 62) on to the two side pieces of obechi sheet wood. Use a craft knife and ruler to cut out the shape, then sand any rough edges using fine-grade sandpaper.

2 Take the front wood piece and chamfer the edge of one long side to an angle of 60 degrees using fine-grade sandpaper (see Basic Techniques page 12).

3 Take the double column and cut where shown to make a drawer knob. Sand the knob and the remaining wood pieces smooth using fine-grade sandpaper. Use a dark brown shoe polish to colour all of the wooden components (see page 12).

4 Take the side wood pieces and position so they are a mirror image of each other. Transfer the ledge measurements from page 62 on to each piece, then position and glue the two top supports into place.

5 Take the base wood piece and mark ⅛in from one short side edge. Position and glue the front support on the line so there is a ⅛in gap between the outside edge of the base and the front support.

6 Position the base as shown. Place the two sides beside the base (ledges facing), together with the back wood piece and glue the three pieces on to the outside edges of the base.

7 Fix the brass handle centrally on to the top wood piece by inserting one ⅛in long brass pin into each hole at the side of the handle through into the wood. Glue the construction on top of the coal box.

8 Take the front wood piece and position it so the chamfered edge faces forwards and downwards. Mark ⅛in from the front long edge and centrally position and glue the wooden knob into place. Once dry, check it slots into the front of the box.

9 To make the hook at the back of the box, cut an eye pin to measure ¼in long and use pliers to slightly open the eye of the pin. Mark ⅛in down from the back of the coal box and drill a hole centrally using a ¹⁄₃₂in drill bit and glue the eye pin into place.

10 To make the scoop, fold the brass sheet in half. Trim the side edges to a slight angle as shown. Make a hole in the top of the folded sheet using a ¹⁄₃₂in drill bit. Take the length of brass wire and secure the end into the hole using superglue gel. Once dry, curve the sides into the shape of a scoop.

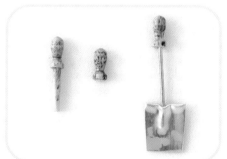

11 To make the handle for the scoop, remove the straight end from the belaying pin using mitre cutters. Use a ¹⁄₃₂in drill bit and drill a hole into the flat end of the pin. Dab the end of the wire with superglue gel and insert it into the pin handle.

12 When the scoop is not in use, insert the brass rod into the hook at the back of the box. Traditionally, coal boxes were lined with metal but this is not included in this project. Instead, dry brush the inside with black acrylic paint and when dry, fill with coal.

Tip

An alternative to the brass sheet used for the handle and coal scoop is the malleable metal of a tomato purée tube which is brass coloured on the inside of the tube. Model railway coal is ideal for filling the coal box.

Festive Silk Bows

Perfectly formed tiny bows can be made using silk ribbon and a home-made bow maker. Silk bows often provide the finishing touch not only to some of the Christmas projects in this chapter but also to many home and personal accessories. Silk ribbon is available in a range of colours and widths and is preferable to satin ribbon as it is finer and more manageable. The instructions are for a right-handed person, so reverse if you are left-handed.

You will need

1/4in thick wood,
  3in x 2 1/2in approximately

Two 3/8in hooks

3mm width silk ribbon for the bows

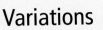

Variations

Depending on the width of the silk ribbon, you can vary the size of the hooks and the distance apart. For 2mm silk ribbon the hooks should be 1/4in apart. For 5mm silk and organdie ribbon they should be 1/2in apart. The same method can be used to make other delicate bows out of threads, string and raffia.

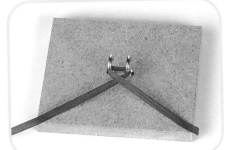

1 To make the bow maker, drill two 1/16in holes into the wooden block so they are in line with each other and 3/8in apart. Screw the hooks into the drilled holes with the openings facing the same way.

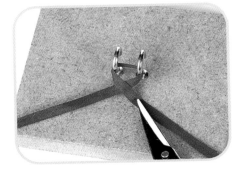

2 Take the silk ribbon and rest it in the openings of the hooks, leaving 2in at one end to work with and the excess at the other end. It doesn't matter how long the excess ribbon is, just work directly from the spool or length of ribbon to avoid wastage.

3 Cross the ribbon in front of the hooks by bringing the short end over the top of the excess ribbon, so each end changes sides.

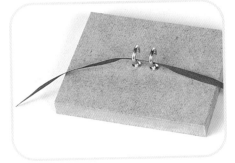

4 At this stage you will need a tool like the small pair of scissors shown. Hold the ribbon in one hand and scissors in the other.

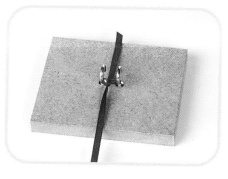

5 Use the point of the scissors to push the short end piece beneath, through the gap in the hooks and underneath the ribbon which is held in the hook openings.

6 Hold the ribbon and gently pull each end, so each end is flat and vertical in front of you.

7 Bring the short end piece of ribbon over the top of the ribbon held in the hooks and hold to your left-hand side whilst taking the opposite end to the right-hand side.

8 Ease the excess ribbon underneath the short end of silk ribbon to form a small loop and hold as shown above.

9 Tuck the short end of the ribbon up and through the silk ribbon loop. Pull each end to centralize and tighten the knot in between the two hooks.

10 Slide the bow off the hooks and trim the ribbon ends to an angle and to the length required.

Tip

You could display Edwardian Christmas cards on a length of 3mm wide silk ribbon, topped with a bow. Christmas card catalogues contain tiny modern and antique images which may be used. Some are small enough to be used as they are, while others may need to be reduced on a photocopier.

Tree Decorations

Decorated Christmas trees are a German tradition dating back to the 16th century. At first the evergreen trees were decorated with fruit, nuts and home-made gifts, but by the beginning of the Victorian era it was the custom to decorate them with ornaments, candles and confectionery. By the 1870s imitation trees were on sale, together with manufactured decorations.

You will need

For the baubles:
Gold-plated head pins

5mm diameter round plastic
  or glass beads

1mm gold-plated crimp beads

34-gauge gold-plated jewellery wire

Round-nosed pliers

For the beaded ornaments:
Seed beads, size 15

34-gauge gold-plated jewellery wire

For the icicles:
Silver-plated head pins

1cm long silver-twisted bugle beads

1mm silver-plated crimp beads

34-gauge silver-plated jewellery wire

For the metal ornaments:
Aluminium foil from
  a foil food container

Mini star paper punch

2mm diameter flat-backed crystals

34-gauge silver-plated jewellery wire

Superglue gel

Baubles

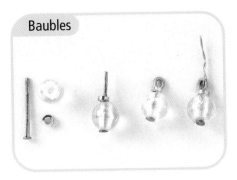

Cut a gold-plated head pin to $^{7}/_{16}$in long. Thread the 5mm round bead, followed by the crimp bead on to the head pin. Use round-nosed pliers to bend the end of the wire into a loop. Attach the baubles to the tree using 34-gauge gold-plated jewellery wire.

Beaded Ornaments

Cut a 2in length of gold-plated jewellery wire. Thread 15 beads on to the centre of the wire and twist the ends of the wire together so the beads form a loop. Trim the end of the twisted wire to $^{5}/_{8}$in long and use to attach the ornament to the Christmas tree.

Icicles

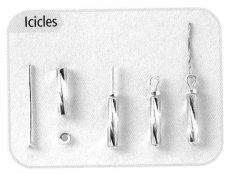

Cut a silver-plated head pin to measure $^{5}/_{8}$in long. Thread a bugle bead on to the head pin, followed by a crimp bead. Use round-nosed pliers to bend the end of the wire into a loop. Attach the icicle to the tree using 34-gauge silver-plated jewellery wire.

Metal Ornaments

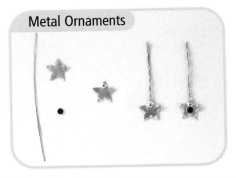

Punch a star shape out of aluminium foil. Use a pin to pierce a hole through the top of the star, thread it on to a 2in length of wire and twist the ends. Use superglue gel to glue a crystal on to the centre of the star and trim the end of the wire to $^{3}/_{4}$in long.

Christmas Fairy

The Christmas fairy evolved from the Christmas angel during the middle of the 18th century. They were first made by German toymakers and were simply frocked dolls with gauze wings and wands. The smaller fairy dolls hung from the branches of the Christmas tree, whilst the larger dolls stood at the foot of the tree. It was not until the mid 20th century that smaller cone-shaped fairies were made to sit on the top of the tree.

You will need

Round natural wood bead, 4mm diameter

Cocktail stick, $^3/_8$in length

Two small pale pink flower stamens

Cream paper ribbon, two $^1/_2$in x $^1/_2$in pieces

Cream bunka (lampshade fringing), 2in length

5mm width cream organdie ribbon

28-gauge silver-plated wire, $^1/_2$in length

Tiny confetti silver star

Water-based acrylic paints

Fine paintbrush

Tacky glue

Variation

Change the wings, substituting the organdie ribbon bow with a pretty pink paper ribbon heart.

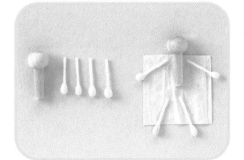

1 Glue the bead on to the end of the cocktail stick and cut the flower stamens to $^1/_4$in long for the arms and legs. Take the paper ribbon and spread tacky glue over one side of each piece (creases running vertically). Position each of the components on top of one piece as shown.

2 Press the other square of paper ribbon on top and leave to dry. Cut the sandwiched section of paper ribbon into shape with small, sharp scissors. Paint the facial features using water-based acrylic paints and a very fine paintbrush.

3 Make the hair from bunka, fraying and curling the bunka by pulling a thread at the end of the braid. Apply a thin layer of tacky glue over the top of the head, lay the frayed bunka along the hairline first and then cover the top of the head in an even layer.

4 Make a bow with the organdie ribbon following the instructions on page 54. Trim the ends and glue on to the fairy's back. Make a wand by gluing a tiny confetti star to the top of a $^1/_2$in length of silver-plated wire. Glue the wand to the front of the fairy's hand.

Stocking and Presents

The giving of gifts to celebrate pagan festivals dates back to ancient times. St Nicholas is associated with gifts at Christmas time and also with the tradition of hanging up a stocking. During the Victorian era, stockings were mostly home-made or an old sock, however, by the end of the 19th century commercially made fabric and paper stockings began to appear in shops.

You will need

For the stocking:
Red and cream paper ribbon

White paper for photocopying

Tacky glue

For the presents:
Small blocks of wood

Paper ribbon in a variety of colours

Metallic thread

Tacky glue

Variation

Tinsel originated in France during the 16th century to embellish military uniforms. It was first used to adorn Christmas trees during the Victorian era. Use lengths of miniature tinsel or tinsel pipe cleaners to decorate your tree and presents. See also the Christmas candlesticks on page 37.

Stocking

1 Photocopy and cut out the stocking template on page 62. Place the template on top of a folded piece of red paper ribbon, creases running vertically, and cut to shape. Cut a 1in x $^{1}/_{16}$in piece of red ribbon, loop it over and glue it to the top of one of the stocking pieces.

2 Glue the edges of the two stocking pieces together. Cut four $^{3}/_{4}$in x $^{1}/_{2}$in pieces of cream paper ribbon and glue on to each side of the stocking as shown. Once dry, trim to shape. Cut a 1$^{3}/_{4}$in x $^{3}/_{16}$in length of cream paper ribbon and glue around the top of the stocking.

Presents

1 Cut a piece of paper ribbon to fold around a small rectangular wooden block (creases to run with the longest length of the block) – the block size shown is $^{7}/_{8}$in x $^{3}/_{8}$in x $^{1}/_{8}$in. Trim the sides to the height of the block and then glue the block on to the paper.

2 Wrap the paper around the wood, using tacky glue to secure. Crease the side flaps, fold over and glue neatly on to the end of the block. Tie metallic thread around the wrapped parcel to provide the finishing touch.

Home-made Decorations

In the run up to Christmas, an Edwardian child's nursery would be a hive of activity, cutting, gluing and making decorations for the home. Overseen by Nanny, coloured paper chains made from gummed strips of paper would adorn the nursery ceiling and walls. Crackers were introduced during the mid 19th century and children delighted in making and filling them with sweets.

You will need

For the paper chains:
2mm width quilling paper in a selection of colours

$^1/_8$in diameter hardwood dowel

Tacky glue

For the crackers:
Red and gold paper ribbon

$^1/_8$in diameter hardwood dowel:
$^1/_4$in lengths for cracker centres
two 1in lengths for removable cracker forms

34-gauge gold-plated jewellery wire

Tacky glue

Variation

You can easily modernize the crackers by decorating them with tiny confetti shapes.

Paper Chains

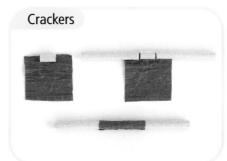

1 Take a strip of quilling paper and cut it into $^5/_8$in lengths. Repeat with the remaining strips of paper. Wind a strip around the dowel to make the first ring and use a small amount of tacky glue to secure the end.

2 Remove the ring from the dowel and thread a different coloured strip of paper into the ring. Rest the dowel next to the previous ring, wind the new strip around the dowel to make the second ring and glue to secure the end. Repeat using the remaining strips to create a long chain.

Crackers

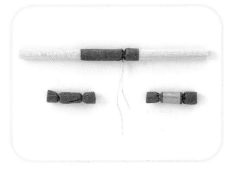

1 Cut a piece of red paper ribbon $^3/_4$in square and glue a short wood dowel piece centrally to the top of the paper (creases running horizontally). Place the forms on either side, roll the paper around all three wood pieces and glue to secure the end of the paper.

2 Take a 2in length of wire and position between the dowel centre and a form. Using pliers, twist the wires to gather the paper. Trim off excess wire, remove the form and repeat on the opposite end. Glue a $^1/_2$in x $^3/_{16}$in piece of gold paper around the centre.

Garland

Before Christianity, evergreen plants were used in pagan celebrations to symbolize the rising sun after the winter solstice. Christians believed evergreens to be symbolic of the eternal life of Jesus and have used them used to decorate homes and churches at Christmas time. Evergreens such as pine, spruce and fir were, and still are, formed into wreaths and garlands and decorated with nuts, fruit and flowers.

You will need

Evergreen garland or pipe cleaners

Centre (reed) cane size 000, 4in length

34-gauge gold-plated wire

Two 3mm width silk ribbon bows (see instructions on page 54)

Dried allspice berries

Coriander seeds

Black and yellow mustard seeds

White peppercorns

Antique pine and light oak water-based wood stain

Tacky glue

Variation

Make a 1¼in diameter wreath following the same instructions. For a more modern alternative, paint some of the seeds with gold paint before decorating.

1 Use wire cutters to cut a length of evergreen garland or pipe cleaner approximately 7in long. Bend into the shape shown in the photograph above.

2 Take another length of evergreen and wind around the garland shape to thicken it. This may need to be repeated depending on the original thickness of the evergreen garland/pipe cleaners.

3 To make cinnamon sticks, take the centre cane and soak in warm water for a few minutes, then pull straight, weigh down each end and leave to dry. Stain with a mix of antique pine and light oak wood stain and once dry cut into ³⁄₈in lengths.

4 Take three cinnamon sticks and bundle together, winding wire around the centre to hold in place. Trim the end of the wire leaving ¹⁄₈in protruding for securing into the garland. Decorate the garland with the sticks, seeds, peppercorns, dried berries and bows.

Templates

Reproduce colour templates either by colour photocopying or by scanning
into a computer and printing out on photo-quality card or paper.

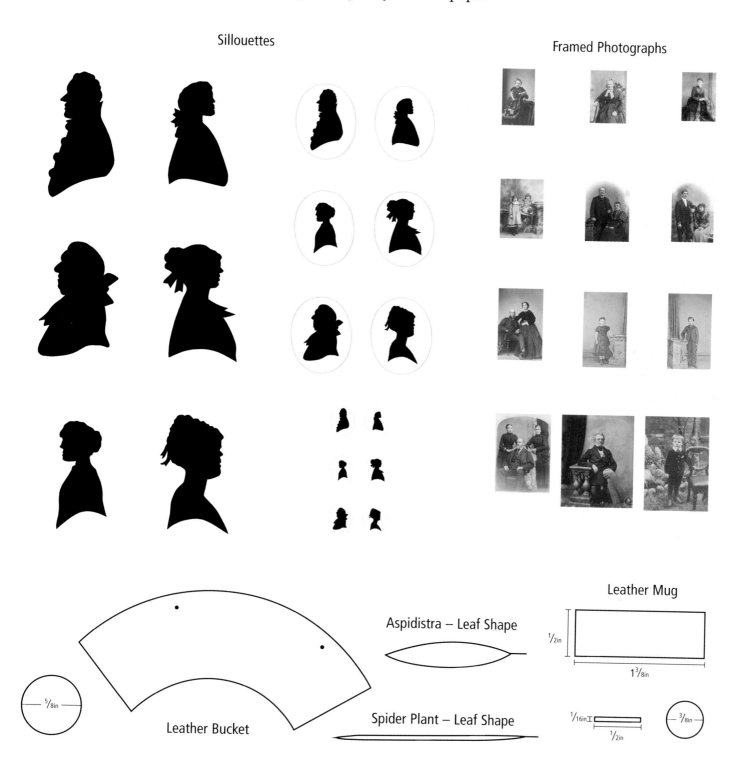

Sillouettes

Framed Photographs

Leather Mug

Aspidistra – Leaf Shape

Leather Bucket

Spider Plant – Leaf Shape

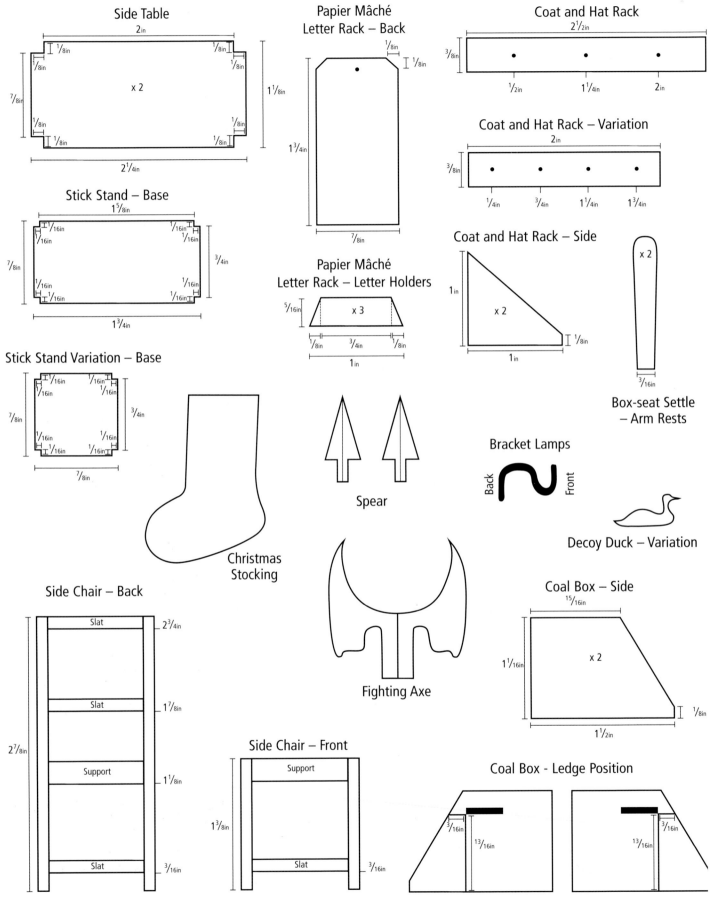

Side Table

Stick Stand – Base

Stick Stand Variation – Base

Papier Mâché Letter Rack – Back

Papier Mâché Letter Rack – Letter Holders

Christmas Stocking

Spear

Fighting Axe

Coat and Hat Rack

Coat and Hat Rack – Variation

Coat and Hat Rack – Side

Bracket Lamps

Decoy Duck – Variation

Box-seat Settle – Arm Rests

Coal Box – Side

Coal Box - Ledge Position

Side Chair – Back

Side Chair – Front

Suppliers

UK

Bead Exclusive
Nixon House, 119–121, Teignmouth
Road, Torquay, Devon TQ1 4HA
tel: 01803 322000
www.beadexclusive.com
For beads and jewellery findings

CelCrafts
Springfield House, Gate Helmsley,
York YO41 1NF
tel: 01759 371447
www.celcrafts.co.uk
*For cold porcelain, paper-covered wire
and floral tape*

Country Treasures
Rose Cottage, Dapple Heath,
Admaston, Nr Rugeley, Staffordshire
WS15 3PG
tel: 01889 500652
For aluminium and paper dinner plates

Dolls House Holidays
Wells Cottage, 204 Main Road,
Milford, Stafford ST17 0UN
tel: 01785 664659
For mitre cutters

Evie's Crafts
79 Dale Street, Milnrow, Rochdale,
Lancs OL16 3NJ
tel: 01706 712489
*For paper punches, peel-off motifs,
quilling paper and quilling tools*

Fine Design
21 Shawley Crescent, Epsom
Downs, Surrey KT18 5PQ
tel: 01737 210886
For the ginger cat (page 20)

Jane Harrop
4 Buckingham Road, Poynton,
Cheshire SK12 1JH
tel: 01625 873117
www.janeharrop.co.uk
*For belaying pins, double columns,
centre cane (reed cane), paper ribbon,
pastel paper, stamens, 3mm eyelets,
tacky glue, antique pine and medium
oak water-based wood stain and
3-D gloss varnish*

Jennifer's of Walsall
51 George Street, Walsall,
West Midlands, WS1 1RS
tel: 01922 623382
www.jennifersofwalsall.co.uk
*For obechi wood, spindles, hardware,
tools, plastic mirrors and polymer clay*

Jojays
Moore Road, Bourton-on-the-Water,
Gloucestershire GL54 2AZ
tel: 01451 810081
www.jojays.co.uk
For hardware and tools

Little Trimmings
PO Box 2267, Reading, RG4 8WG
tel: 0118 9473155
www.littletrimmings.com
*For small-scale haberdashery, canvas,
waxed thread and miniature tinsel*

Susan Lee
8 Springfields, Tetbury,
Gloucestershire GL8 8EN
tel: 01666 505936
www.susan-lee-miniatures.com
For the Victorian shoes (page 39)

Salopian Miniatures
50 Willowfield, Woodside, Telford
TF7 5NT
tel: 01952 581101
For tools and accessories

Tee Pee Crafts
28 Holborn Drive, Mackworth,
Derby DE22 4DX
tel: 01332 332772
www.teepeecrafts.co.uk
*For egg-decorating findings, filigrees,
beads, brass tube, silk and organdie
ribbon, water-slide transfers, peel-off
motifs, bunka and tinsel*

Wood Supplies
Monkey Puzzle Cottage,
53 Woodmansterne
Lane, Wallington,
Surrey SM6 0SW
tel: 020 8669 7266 (eves)
For jelutong wood

US

Cane and Reed
Box 762, Manchester, CT 06045
tel: 800-646-6586
www.caneandreed.com
For round reed cane

Dick Blick Art Materials
PO Box 1267, Galesburg, IL
61402-1267
tel: 800-828-4548
www.dickblick.com
For tools and paper punches

General Bead
371 National City Blvd, National
City, CA 91950-1110
tel: 1-619-336-0100
www.genbead.com
*For beads, jewellery findings and
filigrees*

Happy Hobby Shop
7125 N. 76th Street, Milwaukee, WI
53223
tel: 414-461-6013
www.happyhobby.com
*For tools, glue, bass wood and
brass tube*

Marivi's
9953 S.W.142 Avenue, Miami,
FL33186
tel: 305 388-0010
www.marivis.com
*For cold porcelain and cake-decorating
supplies*

Nature Coast Hobbies, Inc
6773 S. Hancock Road, Homosassa,
Florida 34448
tel: 352-628-3990
www.naturecoast.com
*For belaying pins, double columns
and tools*

Rose's Doll House
12750 W. Capitol Drive,
Brookfield, WI 53005
tel: 262-373-0350
www.happyhobby.com
*For a range of hardware,
tools and spindles*

Index

About the author

Jane Harrop started making miniatures as a hobby ten years ago, making and demonstrating the projects at her local miniatures club. Her enthusiasm turned this hobby into her job – she has been teaching adult education classes on making miniatures for the past seven years. Jane sells her work through miniatures fairs to collectors and also presents miniatures workshops. This is her second book for David & Charles, the first being *Dolls House Do-It-Yourself: Toys and Games*. Jane is married with two daughters and lives in Cheshire, UK.

Acknowledgments

Thank you to the following people who have helped make this project possible.

Brian Gordon for the artwork. Alan Denwood and Bob Williams for their support and advice. Joseph W Harrop and Rob Salter for Victorian photographs. Sally Warrington for the Victorian coat. Jean Tipper for the Victorian plant pot. Paul Meredith from Rufford Old Hall and Garth Vincent for historical information.

And finally, thanks to everyone at David & Charles, Lin Clements and Karl Adamson for the photographs.